NEW MENUS FROM SIMCA'S CUISINE

BOOKS BY SIMONE BECK

Mastering the Art of French Cooking,
Volume One
WITH JULIA CHILD AND LOUISETTE BERTHOLLE
1961

Mastering the Art of French Cooking,
Volume Two
WITH JULIA CHILD
1970

Simca's Cuisine
1972

New Menus from
SIMCA'S CUISINE

Simone Beck

IN COLLABORATION WITH

Michael James

Illustrations by Catherine Brandel

HARCOURT BRACE JOVANOVICH

New York and London

Requests for permission to make copies of
any part of the work should be mailed to:
Permissions, Harcourt Brace Jovanovich, Inc.,
757 Third Avenue, New York, N.Y. 10017.

Design: Dorothy Schmiderer

Printed in the United States of America

LIBRARY OF CONGRESS CATALOGING IN PUBLICATION DATA
Beck, Simone.
New menus from Simca's cuisine.
Includes index.
1. Cookery, French.   I. James, Michael,
1950–   joint author.   II. Title.
TX719.B3885   641.5′944   79-1810
ISBN 0-15-165262-7

B C D E

To my dear husband,
Jean Victor Fischbacher,
whose help and knowledge have
inspired and given confidence
to Simca's cuisine for more
than thirty years.

Acknowledgments

There have been many people who have not only encouraged the writing of this book but have, in their way, helped make it possible. Simone Beck wishes to thank the following:

Carol Worsley, of Birmingham, Michigan; Judith Bell, of Minneapolis; Ailene Martin, of Tulsa; Harriet Healy, of Palm Beach—charming friends—for their graciousness and resourcefulness over the years.

John Ferrone, most gallant editor, without whose intuitive decisions this book would never have been conceived or executed.

Richard Olney, consummate cook and creator, whose insights into the true cooking of Provence have been a constant inspiration.

And to one person in particular—generous, devoted, efficient, tireless in the testing and retesting of recipes—Mary Helen DeLong, of Minneapolis, I express my most heartfelt appreciation. My acquaintance with this gentle-spirited and exquisite woman has been one of the most fortunate of my life.

Michael James wishes to thank the following:

The Waring Corporation for their assistance with test kitchen equipment.

Margaret Fox, Bob Lyon, Jan Weimer, Pamela Michels, Shoshanah Dobry, Axel Fabre, and Akiko Matsuo for their willingness in testing and tasting many of the recipes; Catherine Brandel for her lovely artwork and thoughtful nature; Barbara Lemerman for her constancy as friend; Sydel Lemerman, whose kitchen has always seemed like home.

Margrit Biever for her generous and expert counsel on the subject of

California wines; Marion Cunningham, Nina Schneyer, Faviana Olivier, and Jane Benet for having confidence all along.

James and Nancy Vlamis, devoted parents; Billy Cross, devoted friend.

A special appreciation is expressed to Frances Dinkelspiel Green for her extraordinary trust and encouragement over the years.

And of course, to Simca her *haricot vert* is grateful for life.

Contents

Menus with Fish and Shellfish

Menus with Poultry

Menus with Meat

Introduction

I wonder if this new book of menus and recipes will be as much a surprise to my readers as it is to me—for assuredly, my last book, *Simca's Cuisine,* was to have been just that, the last. But I am, after all, very devoted to my *métier,* and this lifetime fondness for food is hard to set aside. Recent years, intended for my retirement, have instead brought me many discoveries about food and ideas for new dishes, and so how could I dream of retiring? The challenge of students, of my friend and present editor, John Ferrone, and the eager presence of my assistant, Michael James, I could not resist, and so once again, I have been persuaded to produce a volume of my cuisine.

I have kept the menu format that seemed to please so many readers of *Simca's Cuisine,* although this time I have organized the menus in a different way—around main dishes. I think so often one says, "Something with chicken would be nice . . . ," and so it is useful to be able to refer to a group of menus featuring poultry—or fish, or meat, or eggs and cheese, depending on your choice. But always, the menus are intended largely as ideas.

For the first time in one of my books, I have used—as an alternate—the metric system of measures, standard in France but still a new dimension for the American cook. I know that it will surely take another whole generation before metrics begin to seem familiar in the United States, and with this I can sympathize. It makes me think of older people in France, for whom the old-fashioned money, *anciens francs,* will always seem the only real currency. And so it might be with measures in America, but part of life is to anticipate change. From a practical point of view, metric measure can be very useful in cooking, particularly because it encourages the use of weights for dry ingredients, which is more accurate than measuring by volume; also, it is more or less the universal language of cooking. While a good scale is not essential to the success of recipes in this book, it will make the whole cooking process more efficient—this I cannot emphasize too much. Where exact translation into metric terms has been awkward, we have given a sensible equivalent. For this reason, the milliliter has not been used, since it is far too meticulous a measure for the kitchen, as most people will agree. What is presented here—with deciliters and fractions of liters—is essentially the system of measurement we use in France.

The opening menus, with main dishes based on cheese and eggs, are the easiest to be found in the whole book. They contain recipes demanding no extraordinary skills or unusual pieces of equipment and should therefore be especially appealing to the less-experienced cook. These are the sort of modest, everyday menus I would serve to my husband and myself for the lighter meal of the day, and they provide the elementary design of the simplest French family meal, which can be embellished, if you like, by adding a soup, a salad, or a cheese course. I should add that a simple meal does not mean a careless one. If a dish looks appealing when it is served, it begins the experience of good eating.

In other chapters there are dressier dishes that are still easy to execute. For me, the *poulet en persillade* is perhaps the most exemplary of these; it is a nicely cooked chicken dish in an interesting sauce ready to be eaten in about one hour. This is the kind of food I have most wished to write of in this book: cuisine tasting very French, yet not at all classic or complicated. The lightly poached leg of lamb with tarragon cream sauce is also very much in this vein, as are the fish fillets steamed on plates, and the turkey breast *à la Champvallon,* a dish in which potatoes bake right along with the meat and its sauce.

While the approach here is toward simple cooking, it does not mean there are no sumptuous menus or desserts to be found—for this would not be truly French. On the contrary, I have included several menus for festive occasions, including one elegant lunch with an elaborate preparation of chicken stuffed with eggplant and mushrooms, long a favorite with my students; and a gala open-air buffet, for which I have planned a braised veal shoulder stuffed with zucchini. From these dishes, you will see that my recent inclinations run more and more toward vegetable stuffings, always lighter, it seems to me, and more interesting than the classic forcemeats. In fact, I have tried to achieve lightness throughout—by eliminating, for example, flour and egg yolks from many of the sauces.

This book could not be complete without the Provençal dishes so dear to me, and indeed, many of the recipes have the touch of this fragrant and sunny province where I live: the *ratatouille* made with rice; the delicate zucchini stuffed with cream cheese and onions; the Provençal hamburgers with tomato sauce; the rustic *aillade d'agneau,* a lamb shoulder stew with garlic—to name just a few. For many of these influences in my cuisine I have especially to thank my close and very gifted friend, Richard Olney.

I must also acknowledge a debt to certain regional American products of which I have recently become fond—maple syrup, avocados, Dungeness crab, even Kentucky bourbon (mint juleps are a favorite drink of mine during the heat of a Mediterranean summer). All these have found their way into recipes for this book, along with my most recent discovery, the macadamia nut, which I first encountered in Hawaii and so feel it is part of my American education. This rich and tender nut is something I find irresistible, and it has inspired me to create several desserts—cakes, custards, and ice cream—as well as a savory cocktail tidbit. The macadamia has a very delicate flavor, and often is more of a *texture* in a dessert, although when toasted its flavor is enhanced. The macadamia is, alas, quite expensive, and so most recipes suggest an alternate of either almonds or pecans.

In perfecting these recipes, Michael and I have worked hard to bring them closer to the everyday repertoire of American cooks, eliminating fussy details and making dishes faster to do, for nowadays even the most dedicated of cooks cannot always spend three or four hours making a meal. Our goal has frequently been helped by the highly popular food processor, an often impressive machine. I must say that I find the sudden commotion over the "new" food processing devices rather amusing when one considers that these machines are really only baby brothers to the formidable *Robot-Coupe* on which European restaurants have depended for years! Still, even if the household version is *le dernier cri,* it is only to the advantage of good cooking, and you will find many of the recipes here adapted to processor technique: the jet brioche dough, my *nouvelle sauce verte* (an herb mayonnaise without egg), and La Hawaiienne (a special macadamia nut cake) are some examples. Naturally, not everyone owns a food processor, and instructions for working with more modest equipment or by hand are generally included.

Nearly every recipe in this book can be prepared in advance up to some point, to be finished or reheated later. Many desserts can be completed hours and often a day in advance, although the fruit tarts will always be better when completed just before serving; as for the sweet souffles, well, they are always worth the bit of last-minute fuss. I have omitted instructions for preheating the oven, which usually encourages overlong heating, certainly an extravagance these days. If you know your oven and allow just enough time for the heat to stabilize at the right temperature, you should have no trouble.

Concluding the book are two supplementary chapters. The first is a special section of desserts, which I hope will please those who love sweets, and especially creating them, as much as I do. Here you will find a dozen hand-picked recipes from my plump dossier—a rich chocolate *Marquise,* a brioche coffee cake with cream and apples, a delicate pear soufflé, and a selection of *petits fours,* among others. Following the desserts is a chapter of basic preparations. Two new pastry doughs that I think my readers will find interesting are *pâte à croustade,* made with whole egg, which is light and flaky; and a delicate, slightly sweet dough, *pâte sublime.* There are also two new quick yeast doughs in this chapter, as well as the *nouvelle sauce verte* mentioned earlier, a tasty fast tomato sauce, and my updated version of *duxelles.*

I have yet to say something about the choice of French and California wines we have offered with each menu. And if anyone is startled at a French person recommending California wines, then I hope he or she is properly ashamed. If wine is good, that is the main thing, and I have been delighted to discover how wonderful the wine of California can be. And why the wines mostly of California's Napa Valley? Well, it is the American wine region I am most acquainted with, a breathtaking place with air and sunshine so beautifully clear that I have happily spent several weeks teaching there in recent years. (I must confess that much of this happiness is due to a certain feeling for the south of

France, which comes to me in the Napa Valley.) California wine *is* different from French wine. I think it is often pointless to try to compare them: there are similarities, sometimes, but not always. The wines, then, that you will find listed here are the French varieties I would serve at my own table in France, or the California ones that might be served if I were preparing these menus in the United States.

I belong with my generation to a more romantic age, to which I am quite attached, and I am sometimes sorry to see how much of this is now being passed by. But I am a modern woman as well where food is concerned, and I have written this book with my thoughts for the marvelous age of cooking in the United States, where there has been a revival of interest in the pleasures of food nicely prepared. It is there, I am beginning to think, that much of the hope for good home-cooking might rest. In France, cooking is apt to be regarded as a profession, or as something menial and associated with an unglamorous domesticity. French people, frequently not interested in cooking, eat in restaurants or take home dishes from the charcuterie or have their own cooks; or they may not eat very well at all. In the United States, where there is less of a tradition for great restaurants than in France, good home-cooking is a necessity, and how happy I have been to work for this result with my American friends. Their dedication to food has only fed my own, and for this I am most profoundly grateful.

Looking back on my career, I can think of few regrets, even though it has been an unlikely profession for the young girl who was once banished by her mother from the family kitchen in Normandy for pleading with the cook to let her bake a cake. *"Mademoiselle Simone, pas dans la cuisine!"* she admonished, for in those days no respectable young girl was to meddle in such tasks. If that extraordinary woman— my mother—and I had suspected the course of my life, I have no doubt it would have astonished us both.

SIMONE BECK

xix

NEW MENUS FROM SIMCA'S CUISINE

Menus with Eggs and Cheese

MAIN DISHES:

Les oeufs en meurette

Gnocchi de semoule gratinés

Les omelettes en sandwich

Flan aux deux fromages et à l'aneth

La pizza Jeannette

Un déjeuner intime
AN INTIMATE LUNCH FOR 6

Les oeufs en meurette
POACHED EGGS WITH VEGETABLES
AND RED WINE

Purée de haricots verts au beurre
PURÉE OF GREEN BEANS WITH BUTTER

Sorbet à l'orange et au cassis
ORANGE ICE WITH ORANGE PEEL CANDIED
IN BLACK-CURRANT LIQUEUR

Beaujolais—Fleurie / Ridge Lytton
Springs Zinfandel

Un déjeuner intime

I always think it is a practical idea to serve poached eggs to an intimate group of not more than four or five friends or family members who can appreciate their delicacy and the time spent carefully cooking them. The *meurette* sauce for the eggs in this menu is one often used for fish as well, and is a kind of stewed *mirepoix à la bourguignonne*— a base of aromatic vegetables concentrated with red wine. The eggs themselves are also poached in the red wine, which later becomes part of the reduction, and are served on crisp toasted bread with the dark wine sauce poured over.

To simplify the dish, you could omit the toast altogether—although, apart from having a nice texture, they make the eggs easy to transfer from the platter to the plates—in which case it would be easier to serve the eggs on individual plates. As for the eggs themselves, if you are shy about poaching them, simple fried eggs, lightly basted with butter, will do quite nicely. But whether you do the eggs poached or in a skillet, the yolks should remain soft and slightly runny, to combine with the sauce in a delicious way when the dish is eaten.

The *purée de haricots verts* is something Richard Olney made one day at my house. Richard is a wonderful friend and one of the most creative people in the kitchen that I know; his food always has an extraordinary taste. His idea for this purée is something I find very useful for the American string bean, which, *entre nous,* is not quite like the French one—sometimes a little too big and tough, although I have, on occasion, found nice tender beans. But when you can find only overgrown beans, one of the best preparations for them is a purée. With the rice in this recipe (only a small amount) the purée has a nice body, not at all watery or thin, which the beans alone would be. And yet it is still a light dish.

A fruit ice is always a nice finish to a lunch, and the *sorbet à l'orange et au cassis,* with its contrast of black currant and orange, makes a pretty and refreshing complement to the meal. It is also very good for the digestion.

X

Les oeufs en meurette

POACHED EGGS WITH VEGETABLES
AND RED WINE

For 6:

6 tablespoons (85 g) butter
1 medium-sized carrot, peeled and diced
2 medium-sized shallots, peeled and minced
¼ pound (115 g) unsliced bacon, diced
1 bottle good red wine

Bouquet garni—parsley, fresh or dried thyme, bay leaf
6 slices *pain de mie au lait,* page 215
6 eggs
1 teaspoon potato starch
1 teaspoon salt
Freshly ground pepper
A few sprigs of parsley

Melt 2 tablespoons (30 g) butter in a skillet and stir in the diced carrots, shallots, and bacon. Cook gently over medium heat for 8 to 10 minutes, stirring from time to time, then pour in 1 cup (¼ L) of the wine, and add the *bouquet garni.* Allow to simmer over low heat until the wine is reduced to a tablespoon or two and the vegetables are tender, for about 20 minutes. Set aside.

Trim the crusts from the slices of bread and toast them on both sides under a medium-hot broiler. Spread a bit of the remaining butter on the toast, then arrange on an ovenproof serving dish.

5

Put the remaining wine in a small saucepan and bring it to a simmer. Poach the eggs, one or two at a time, by breaking them individually into a small custard cup (I use a demitasse cup) and then slipping them down the side of the pan into the simmering liquid. Spoon the egg white back over the egg yolk to help the egg hold its shape, and continue cooking the eggs until the white is just firm and the yolk still soft, for 4 to 5 minutes. (Eggs normally take longer to cook in wine than in water.) As they are done, use a skimmer to lift them onto a paper towel to drain, where they may wait for 20 to 30 minutes at room temperature.

Boil the poaching liquid rapidly down to 1 cup (¼ L). Dissolve the starch in a teaspoon or two of cold water and whisk it into the hot liquid, stirring over heat until it thickens slightly, then add this to the shallot and carrot glaze in the skillet. Stir the sauce over heat with a wooden spatula, scraping the sides and bottom of the pan to deglaze it thoroughly. Remove the *bouquet garni* and season.

When ready to serve, trim the eggs, if necessary, then arrange them on the toast, and heat in a 300°F (150°C) oven for 5 to 7 minutes. Reheat the sauce and off the heat swirl in the remaining butter. Correct the seasoning and spoon over the warm eggs. Serve garnished with the parsley.

Purée de haricots verts au beurre
PURÉE OF GREEN BEANS WITH BUTTER

For 6:

3 tablespoons long-grain white rice

2 pounds (900 g) fresh green beans, trimmed

6 tablespoons (85 g) butter, at room temperature

¼ cup (½ dL) heavy cream

Salt

Freshly ground pepper

Add the rice to 3 quarts (3 L) of boiling water and simmer it for 12 minutes, until it is just beginning to be tender, stirring once or twice. Then add the green beans, return to a boil, and add 2 tablespoons salt. Continue to boil rapidly until they are very tender, for 5 to 10 minutes, depending on the size and quality of the beans. Drain and refresh the beans and rice under cold running water, then set aside to drain thoroughly.

Purée the green beans and rice in two lots in a food processor, whipping until you have a fine purée, or else put through the medium and then fine disks of a food mill. Add 2 teaspoons of salt, and pepper, to taste, and turn into a saucepan, where the purée may wait for 3 to 4 hours at room temperature covered with plastic wrap; it can also be made the day before and refrigerated.

When you are ready to serve, stir over medium-high heat to warm thoroughly, then stir in the butter and cream and correct the seasoning.

Sorbet à l'orange et au cassis

ORANGE ICE WITH ORANGE PEEL CANDIED
IN BLACK-CURRANT LIQUEUR

For 6:

5 sweet, juicy oranges
½ cup (1 dL) *crème* or *sirop de cassis* (black-currant liqueur or syrup)
1 tablespoon powdered sugar

1 egg white
⅓ cup (65 g) granulated sugar
Juice of 1 lemon
Sprigs of fresh mint

Peel off thin strips of the zest of one of the oranges, using a vegetable peeler, and cut into fine julienne. Simmer with the *cassis* and 5 tablespoons water for 15 to 20 minutes, until the peel is tender and the liquid has reduced to a light syrup. Transfer to a small bowl and refrigerate.

7

Using a small, sharp knife, remove the orange segments from the peeled orange and one additional orange by cutting away the peel and white pith and then slicing between each membrane. Squeeze any juice from the orange pulp into a bowl. Place the segments in another bowl and sprinkle with the powdered sugar and with a few drops of *cassis,* if you wish. Put in the refrigerator to chill. Slice the other three oranges in half and squeeze out their juice, being careful not to break the skins. Add the juice to the bowl; you should have about 1½ cups (3½ dL) in all. Using a teaspoon, remove all of the pulp from the orange halves and discard it. Place the orange cups on a plate, trimming the bottoms slightly with a knife to help them sit flat if necessary, and then set in the freezer.

Beat the egg white slightly with a fork, then add it to the orange juice, along with the granulated sugar and juice of the lemon. Beat the mixture together briefly and pour it into any shallow metal container to help it freeze faster; a couple of cake pans or ice trays would work well. Place the mixture in the freezer and allow it to nearly set, for about 1½ hours. Remove the *sorbet* from the freezer and either beat it with an electric beater or whip it in a food processor. It should be smooth and fluffy.

The *sorbet* is now ready to be spooned into the chilled orange cups, and may be served at once or held up to an hour in the freezer. If you wish to wait longer, return the ice to the pan and allow it to freeze again. When you are ready to serve, either turn the mixture into a bowl, chop it up with a metal spoon, and beat it with the mixer until it is fluffy and smooth again (this may take 1 or 2 minutes), or whip it again in the food processor. Then spoon it into the cups.

To garnish, place two or three of the fresh orange segments on top of the ice in each cup and spoon on some of the orange peel with its syrup. Serve with a sprig of fresh mint.

Un repas sans façon

A MEAL WITHOUT FUSS FOR 6 TO 8

✕

Gnocchi de semoule gratinés

SEMOLINA DUMPLINGS GRATINÉED
WITH CHEESE

Courgettes à la Campanette

ZUCCHINI SIMMERED IN BROTH
AND SAUTÉED IN BUTTER

Pommes grand'mère de Hilo

UNMOLDED APPLE CUSTARD WITH
MACADAMIA-NUT BRITTLE

Mâcon Blanc / Beaulieu Chablis

Un repas sans façon

A MEAL WITHOUT FUSS FOR 6 TO 8

This is a cozy menu for a chilly day, and one that is child's play to prepare and serve. The dish with semolina dumplings is really one of the best versions of gnocchi that I know. Made only of semolina and milk (no *pâte à choux*), and rolled in cheese, it is uncomplicated and lighter than the traditional one made with potato. The dumplings are also excellent reheated the next day in a sauce Mornay, and instructions for this follow the recipe.

The *courgettes* in their butter sauce are a tasty accompaniment and can really be cut into any shape—into rounds, strips, or cubes. If you don't have any homemade chicken broth, make some from chicken bouillon cubes, and the dish will still be very good. The fresh or dried tarragon sprinkled on at the end brings a most subtle perfume to the taste of the zucchini.

The *pommes grand'mère de Hilo* reflects my fascination with the macadamia nut, which I discovered on a recent visit to Hawaii. How tender it is when it is cooked! Not at all like the almond, although either one would be very good in this dessert. (And if you wish to save time, you can simply eliminate the brittle altogether and use plain chopped nuts.) The precooking of the apples in this dessert is very important, as it eliminates much of their water, which would otherwise thin out the custard. This method of baking apples can also be useful for many other desserts, including any kind of apple tart.

Gnocchi de semoule gratinés

SEMOLINA DUMPLINGS GRATINÉED
WITH CHEESE

For 6 to 8:

4 cups (1 L) milk
8 tablespoons (115 g) butter
2 teaspoons salt
Freshly ground pepper

Freshly grated nutmeg
1⅓ cups (185 g) semolina
2 cups (180 g) finely grated
    Gruyère or Parmesan cheese

Recommended equipment: A large oval gratin dish

Butter the gratin dish well. In a large saucepan bring the milk, 4 tablespoons (60 g) butter, and the seasonings to a simmer. Stir in the semolina with a wooden spoon and cook for 20 to 25 minutes, stirring constantly, until the mixture is smooth and quite thick. Off heat stir in ½ cup (45 g) cheese, then taste for seasoning. Turn the gnocchi mixture into the prepared dish and firm it in the refrigerator for at least 30 minutes; the mixture can easily wait overnight, covered with plastic wrap.

Turn out of the dish in one large piece, and either slice into 1-inch (2½ cm) squares or triangles; or, using two soup spoons, shape into nice ovals. Place in an overlapping layer in the gratin dish. Sprinkle with the remaining cheese and dot with the last of the butter. The dish may now wait for an hour or two at room temperature before finishing.

Bake in a 450°F (230°C) oven for about 15 minutes, or until the gnocchi begin to brown. To give a crusty finish, you can run them under a hot broiler for a few seconds. Allow the dish to cool for a minute or two before serving.

Gnocchi gratinés, sauce Mornay

SEMOLINA DUMPLINGS WITH CHEESE SAUCE

Any leftover gnocchi are delicious reheated with a rich tomato sauce, such as the one on page 220, or with the sauce Mornay that follows. Either sauce will help keep the dumplings moist during reheating.

Sauce Mornay

For 1½ cups (3½ dL); enough for half of the gnocchi recipe:

1 tablespoon (15 g) butter
1½ tablespoons all-purpose flour
1 cup (¼ L) milk
½ teaspoon salt
Freshly ground pepper
A few grains of freshly grated
  nutmeg

½ cup (45 g) plus 1 or 2
  tablespoons grated Gruyère
  cheese
1 or 2 tablespoons heavy cream, if
  needed

In a saucepan melt the butter over medium heat, stir in the flour, and cook for 1 to 2 minutes. Whisk in the milk all at once, along with the seasonings, and continue whisking until the sauce thickens and is smooth. Off heat stir in ½ cup (45 g) cheese, then taste the sauce for seasoning. If you don't wish to use the sauce immediately, press a piece of plastic wrap directly over its surface and set aside or refrigerate.

Arrange leftover gnocchi in a single layer in a buttered baking dish just large enough to hold them. Rewarm the sauce slightly, thinning it down with the cream if necessary, and pour it over the gnocchi. Sprinkle on the remaining cheese and bake in a 450°F (230°C) oven for 15 to 20 minutes, until lightly browned.

Courgettes à la Campanette

ZUCCHINI SIMMERED IN BROTH
AND SAUTÉED IN BUTTER

For 6 to 8:

3 pounds (1350 g) zucchini,
  washed and trimmed
4 cups (1 L) chicken broth
8 tablespoons (115 g) butter

1½ teaspoons salt
Freshly ground pepper
1 tablespoon chopped fresh
  tarragon or 1 teaspoon dried

Slice the zucchini into strips 2 inches (5 cm) long and ⅛ inch (⅓ cm) thick. Bring the chicken broth to a rapid boil in a large saucepan or skillet and cook the zucchini in two batches for 3 to 4 minutes, until it is just tender. As the zucchini is done, remove it to a dish or tray to cool in a more or less single layer. The squash may now wait for 1 or 2 hours at room temperature before final cooking. The chicken broth may be cooled and then stored for another use.

To finish the zucchini, melt the butter in a large skillet. Add the zucchini with the seasonings and tarragon and toss or stir over high heat for 3 to 4 minutes until it is hot. The zucchini will render its juices slightly as it reheats, making a creamy sauce with the butter. Correct the seasoning, turn into a hot vegetable dish, and serve.

Pommes grand'mère de Hilo

UNMOLDED APPLE CUSTARD WITH
MACADAMIA-NUT BRITTLE

For 6 to 8:

3 ounces (85 g) unsalted
   macadamia nuts (washed of
   their salt if necessary)
⅔ cup (130 g) granulated sugar
1 tablespoon water
1 teaspoon lemon juice
¼ teaspoon baking powder
3 pounds (1350 g) well-flavored
   apples—pippin, Granny
   Smith, or Golden Delicious—
   peeled, cored, and cut into
   ⅛-inch (¼ cm) slices

6 tablespoons (85 g) unsalted
   butter
1 tablespoon cinnamon
1 ounce (30 g) stale bread—even
   a brioche or croissant
4 eggs
Pinch of salt
¼ cup (½ dL) heavy cream
2 tablespoons Calvados or
   Cognac
¼ cup (½ dL) raspberry jam,
   melted and strained

Recommended equipment: A 6-cup (1½ L) metal charlotte mold

Line the bottom of the charlotte mold with waxed paper, and butter
the entire mold. Toast the macadamia nuts on a baking sheet set in the
middle of a 350°F (180°C) oven for 8 to 10 minutes, until they are
golden brown. While they are still warm, bring ⅓ cup (65 g) sugar,
the water, and lemon juice to a boil over high heat in a small saucepan
and allow to caramelize, giving the pan a swirl occasionally. Off heat
stir in the macadamia nuts, using a metal tablespoon, then the baking
powder, which will make the caramel froth and turn creamy. Pour
onto a well-buttered baking sheet and set aside to cool completely;
you may place it in the freezer to hurry this along.

   Butter another large baking sheet and arrange the apples on it in a
flat layer. Dot with the butter, sprinkle with the cinnamon, and bake

in a 375°F (190°C) oven for 20 to 30 minutes, until very tender, stirring once or twice. Set aside to cool.

When the macadamia brittle is cold, remove it from the baking sheet with a metal spatula and chop it coarsely with a knife, or in a food processor, running it on and off. Some of the brittle should retain a bit of texture, rather like kernels of corn. Set aside.

Crush the stale bread into coarse crumbs in the processor or with a rolling pin. Coat the prepared mold with some of the crumbs, and blend the remainder with the macadamia brittle.

In a large bowl beat the eggs with the remaining ⅓ cup (65 g) of sugar, the salt, cream, and Calvados. Stir in the apples. Spoon a third of the apple/custard mixture into the mold and sprinkle on half of the brittle and crumbs. Add half of the remaining custard, another layer of brittle and crumbs, and then the remaining apples. The filled mold may wait for an hour at room temperature. Bake in a 375°F (190°C) oven for about 30 minutes, until the custard has puffed slightly and the sides are set.

Remove to a rack to cool for at least 30 minutes before unmolding. Then run a flexible metal spatula around the sides of the dessert, invert it onto a serving dish, and remove the piece of waxed paper. Brush with the raspberry glaze. Serve either warm or cold, cut into wedges.

Un souper du dimanche soir pour
vider le réfrigérateur

A SUNDAY NIGHT SUPPER FOR 6,
TO EMPTY THE ICEBOX

※

Les omelettes en sandwich
A SANDWICH OF OMELETS, FILLED
WITH SPINACH, CHEESE, TOMATO SAUCE,
AND MUSHROOMS

Salade de pommes de terre composée
POTATO SALAD WITH HERB MAYONNAISE
AND GREENS WITH VINAIGRETTE

Fruits pochés en poncho
APPLES AND PEARS POACHED
IN MAPLE SYRUP AND BOURBON AND
CLOAKED IN PASTRY

Bordeaux rouge du Médoc/Liberty School
Cabernet Sauvignon

Un souper du dimanche soir pour
vider le réfrigérateur

A SUNDAY NIGHT SUPPER FOR 6,
TO EMPTY THE ICEBOX

Every now and then I find my refrigerator simply overflowing with leftovers, and it is usually on Sunday, with the accumulation of the week's family meals and dinner parties. Then it is time to make a clean sweep, and this menu with its stack of filled omelets is the ideal way to do just that. My suggestions for fillings are only an idea, based on what a busy kitchen tends to produce: leftover vegetables, stray bits of cheese, a teacup with the last bit of tomato sauce, one hard-boiled egg. Any kind of filling will really do as long as it will spread and still hold its shape. Since a number of omelets are required, they can be done in advance. And should you not have a dozen eggs on hand, the perfect solution is to do the dish with crêpes instead; instructions for this follow the master recipe. Certainly this is what we might do in wintertime in France, because crêpes use one-third the amount of eggs; winter eggs, while the chickens are molting and laying less often, are quite expensive.

Since the egg dish is so complete in itself, it needs only the company of a *salade composée*. Here I suggest a good potato salad tossed with a special green mayonnaise made without egg, along with a few crunchy salad greens in vinaigrette. You can also add any cooked leftover vegetables that you might have.

The *fruits pochés en poncho* is an amusing dessert, so named because the pastry really does make a kind of poncho or cape over the fruit. The apples and pears are not completely wrapped in pastry because the bottom would only become soggy in the oven. If you like, you can poach the fruit in a simple sugar syrup rather than in the maple syrup, but the maple does give an excellent flavor, and of course the syrup—delicious with the flavors of pear and apple and bourbon —is not lost; save it for breakfast pancakes.

Les omelettes en sandwich

A SANDWICH OF OMELETS, FILLED WITH SPINACH, CHEESE, TOMATO SAUCE, AND MUSHROOMS

For 6 to 8:

For the spinach filling:

1 pound (450 g) fresh spinach, stemmed and washed
2 hard-boiled eggs, peeled
3 tablespoons (45 g) butter
1 tablespoon minced shallots
1 teaspoon salt

Freshly ground pepper
Freshly grated nutmeg
3 tablespoons heavy cream
⅓ cup (70 g) leftover chicken, fish, or ham, cut or broken into small pieces (optional)

For the cheese and fresh herb filling:

1 ounce (30 g) cream cheese, preferably without gum additives
2 tablespoons heavy cream
1 ounce (30 g) good blue cheese
¼ teaspoon salt

Freshly ground pepper
1 tablespoon chopped fresh herbs —chives or tarragon or basil— or ¼ teaspoon dried tarragon
1 tablespoon chopped fresh parsley

For the tomato sauce and mushroom fillings:

3 to 4 tablespoons quick tomato sauce, page 220

½ recipe creamy minced mushrooms, page 219

19

For 6 omelets:

1 dozen eggs	6 tablespoons (85 g) unsalted
1 teaspoon salt	butter
Freshly ground pepper	1 tablespoon chopped fresh
1 tablespoon water	parsley
2 teaspoons Dijon mustard	Sprigs of fresh herbs

Recommended equipment: An 8- to 9-inch (20-23 cm) nonstick skillet; a 12-inch (30 cm) round serving platter

Cook the spinach for 3 to 4 minutes in a large quantity of boiling salted water. Drain and refresh in cold water, then drain again thoroughly and squeeze dry in a strong kitchen towel. Chop fairly fine in a food processor or with a knife. Put the hard-boiled eggs through a fine sieve or through the fine disk of a food mill. In the skillet melt the butter, then add the shallots and sauté them gently for 1 or 2 minutes. Add the spinach to the pan, along with the sieved egg, seasonings, cream, and optional chicken, fish, or ham. Stir over medium heat for 3 or 4 minutes to evaporate most of the excess moisture in the spinach. Taste carefully for seasoning and transfer to a bowl.

Using either a food processor or an electric beater, blend the cream cheese with the cream, blue cheese, seasonings, and herbs. If the mixture is to be used within an hour or two, keep it at room temperature.

Using a fork, break up the eggs with the seasonings, water, and mustard. For each omelet melt 1 tablespoon (15 g) of butter in the same skillet set over medium-high heat and pour in ½ cup (1 dL) of the egg batter. Shake the pan over the heat as you briskly scramble the eggs and then pat them into an even layer, using the back of the fork; after about 10 seconds the eggs should be lightly set yet still creamy. If necessary, cook a few additional seconds to firm the omelet up, then slip unrolled onto a platter. Spread the first omelet with half of the spinach mixture. Continue to stack the next four omelets, spreading with the cheese, tomato sauce, mushrooms, and then the last of the spinach. Top with the sixth omelet, browned side up.

The finished dish may wait for an hour or two at room temperature before serving, although the fresher it is the better it will be. Garnish with the chopped parsley and sprigs of herbs, and cut into wedges.

Variation: Crêpes gypsy. (A sandwich of crêpes, filled with spinach, cheese, tomato sauce, and mushrooms.) Prepare a dozen 8-inch (20 cm) unsweetened crêpes. Arrange in layers, alternating the fillings, until all but one of the crêpes are used up. Top with the last crêpe, garnish with some fresh parsley, and serve tepid, sliced into wedges.

If you wish to serve the *crêpes gypsy* hot with a sauce, they may wait for 2 or 3 hours at room temperature; then heat in a 375°F (190°C) oven for 20 to 25 minutes, topped with the quick tomato sauce (page 220).

Salade de pommes de terre composée

POTATO SALAD WITH HERB MAYONNAISE
AND GREENS WITH VINAIGRETTE

For 6:

2 pounds (900 g) boiling potatoes, well scrubbed
5 tablespoons dry white wine
1 cup (¼ L) *nouvelle sauce verte*, page 217
Salt and freshly ground pepper

12 to 15 leaves of crisp salad greens, such as chicory or romaine
3 tablespoons each olive oil and tasteless salad oil
2 teaspoons vinegar

Cook the potatoes in boiling salted water until they are tender when pierced with a knife. Drain in a colander and set aside. When they have cooled, peel them and cut them into ¼-inch (⅔ cm) slices. Toss gently in a bowl with the wine. When the wine has been absorbed, stir in the *sauce verte*. Correct the seasoning. The salad may now wait for several hours, either at room temperature or in the refrigerator.

At the last minute toss the salad greens with the oils, vinegar, ¼ teaspoon salt, and pepper. Correct the seasoning. Serve the potato salad on the bed of tossed greens.

Fruits pochés en poncho

APPLES AND PEARS POACHED IN MAPLE SYRUP
AND BOURBON AND CLOAKED IN PASTRY

For 6:

3 juicy, ripe pears—Comice or
   Bartlett—with stems, if
   possible
3 tasty apples—Golden Delicious,
   pippin, Granny Smith, etc.

3 cups (¾ L) maple syrup
1 cup (¼ L) bourbon
1 recipe *pâte sublime,* page 213
1 egg plus 1 teaspoon water,
   lightly beaten with a fork

Peel the pears and apples, taking care not to disturb the stems; core the fruit carefully from the bottom and trim slightly, if necessary, to help them sit flat. Bring the maple syrup and the bourbon to a simmer in a medium-sized saucepan. Poach first the pears, and then the apples, for 4 to 8 minutes, turning and basting them with the syrup until they are beginning to be tender when pierced with a knife. The cooking time will depend on the quality and ripeness of the fruit; the apples in general will tend to take longer. Be careful not to overcook. Remove from the pan with a slotted spoon, set on a plate, and refrigerate while you prepare the pastry. Allow the maple syrup to cool.

Roll out one-half of the dough until about ¹⁄₁₆ inch (¼ cm) thick, and cut out three 5-inch (13 cm) circles, using a lid or a plate for a guide. Repeat with the other half of the pastry. You may need to re-assemble and roll out some of the scraps for the last circle or two. Roll out any remaining pastry, cut out 18 leaf shapes, and score a leaf pattern on them with the back of a knife. If the pastry becomes too soft to handle at any point, simply refrigerate it.

When the pears and apples have cooled, place a pastry circle on top of each one, allowing the stem to poke through the center. Mold the pastry gently around the sides of the fruit. Gently brush on some of the egg glaze, then press the leaf shapes into place around the stems of the fruit, adding little pastry leaf stems, if you wish. Brush the surface of the pastry with more of the egg glaze. The fruit may now wait for 3 to 4 hours in the refrigerator, if desired.

When ready to bake, give the pastry a last brushing of glaze, then place the fruit on a baking sheet. Bake in a 400°F (205°C) oven for 20 to 25 minutes, until the pastry is golden brown and cooked through. Cool the fruit for a few moments at room temperature before presenting in a serving dish or in individual bowls. Pass a little of the maple poaching syrup, and save the rest for another use. The dessert is best served warm, and can be reheated for 10 minutes in a 350°F (180°C) oven to crisp the pastry.

Un repas nourrissant pour amis affamés

A NOURISHING MEAL FOR FAMISHED FRIENDS,
FOR 6 TO 8

🌾

Flan aux deux fromages et à l'aneth
RICH CHEESE CUSTARD WITH DILL

Choux de Bruxelles à la Crécy
BRUSSELS SPROUTS WITH CARROTS
COOKED IN BUTTER

Pouding aux pruneaux et aux abricots
BREAD PUDDING WITH DRIED PRUNES
AND APRICOTS

Sancerre/Robert Mondavi Fumé Blanc

Un repas nourrissant pour amis affamés

This is a menu for friends or one's family when appetites are keen from a bracing walk or from a long day at the office. It is also the kind of meal I would serve to travelers arriving late and yearning for something homecooked. The *flan aux deux fromages* is a substantial dish, full of eggs, cheese and cream, and together with the Brussels sprouts and the bread pudding, makes a good and filling meal.

There are no special skills—what we call *tour de main*—involved in this menu. The main dish is made without pastry, only a very light crust of stale bread crumbs and butter; for the custard you could use one of the very good American blue cheeses—a creamy Oregon blue, for instance. I have included Brussels sprouts in the menu because they are a very hearty vegetable and can be delicious when they are not overcooked. They are garnished with minced carrots cooked in butter, which makes a pleasing contrast of both color and flavor.

The dessert is a traditional kind of Alsatian *pouding* made with bread and fruit. When my husband Jean was a boy, it was his favorite dessert; this was, I suppose, before his discovery of chocolate. The pudding is a dessert that can keep for several days while even improving in flavor.

𝒳

Flan aux deux fromages et à l'aneth

RICH CHEESE CUSTARD WITH DILL

For 6 to 8:

¾ cup (85 g) dry white bread
    crumbs
2 tablespoons (30 g) butter, at
    room temperature
2 ounces (60 g) blue cheese
1 pound (450 g) cream cheese,
    preferably without gum
    additives

3 eggs
1⅓ cups (3¼ dL) sour cream
1 teaspoon salt
Freshly ground pepper
1 tablespoon chopped fresh dill
    or 1 teaspoon dried
¼ teaspoon *herbes de Provence*
    (see page 220)

Recommended equipment: A 10-inch (25 cm) pie plate

Thoroughly butter the pie plate. Press the bread crumbs firmly into all surfaces of the buttered pan. Set in the refrigerator.

Blend together the butter with the blue cheese and the cream cheese, using the food processor or an electric beater. Then blend in the eggs, ⅔ cup (1½ dL) of the sour cream, and the seasonings and herbs. Taste the mixture for seasoning. You may prepare this several hours in advance (or the night before) and keep it in the refrigerator.

When you are ready to bake the dish, pour the cheese mixture into the pan and set in a 375°F (190°C) oven. Bake for 25 to 30 minutes, or until the custard has puffed slightly and just set; if the custard was cold when it went into the oven, it will probably take the full 30 minutes.

Remove from the oven, spread on the remaining sour cream in an even layer, and return the dish to the oven for 10 minutes to finish cooking. Set on a rack to cool until you are ready to serve. While it may be eaten cold, the flan is really best served warm and can be reheated for 15 to 20 minutes in a 300°F (150°C) oven. Serve in slices directly from the pie plate.

Choux de Bruxelles à la Crécy

BRUSSELS SPROUTS WITH CARROTS
COOKED IN BUTTER

For 6 to 8:

2 pounds (900 g) fresh Brussels
   sprouts, trimmed (and washed
   if necessary)
Salt
½ pound (225 g) carrots,
   peeled
6 tablespoons (85 g) butter

½ cup (1 dL) water
¼ cup (½ dL) dry white wine
1 teaspoon *herbes de Provence*
   (see page 220)
Freshly ground pepper
Finely chopped fresh parsley

Plunge the Brussels sprouts into boiling water, return to a boil, and add 2 to 3 tablespoons salt. Cook at a rapid boil until they are just tender when pierced with a knife—for about 6 to 8 minutes. Drain, refresh briefly in cold water, then set aside to drain thoroughly.

Slice the peeled carrots in half, then cut them into ½-inch (1¼ cm) lengths and mince fine either in a food processor or with a knife. Melt the butter in a large skillet and stir in the carrots, along with the water, wine, ½ teaspoon salt, and the herbs. Simmer, uncovered, over medium heat, stirring from time to time until the carrots are tender and the liquid has mostly evaporated, for about 15 to 20 minutes. The finished carrots and Brussels sprouts may now wait for 3 or 4 hours at room temperature.

When you are ready to serve, warm the carrots in the skillet, then add the Brussels sprouts, 1½ teaspoons salt, and pepper to taste. Stir or toss gently for 3 or 4 minutes over medium-high heat until hot. Correct the seasoning. Turn into a hot vegetable dish and sprinkle with a little chopped parsley.

Pouding aux pruneaux et aux abricots

BREAD PUDDING WITH DRIED PRUNES
AND APRICOTS

For 6:

½ pound (225 g) pitted prunes
4 ounces (115 g) dried apricots
1 cup (¼ L) good red wine or
    strong tea
1 teaspoon cinnamon
4 ounces (115 g) fresh white
    bread, crust removed, and
    broken into small pieces
⅔ cup (1½ dL) milk

1 cup (190 g) granulated sugar
4 tablespoons (60 g) unsalted
    butter
Finely grated zest of 1 orange
3 eggs, lightly beaten
3 tablespoons dark rum or
    imported kirsch (optional)
¼ cup (60 g) sliced almonds

Recommended equipment: a 1½-quart (1½ L) Pyrex casserole or a medium-sized oval gratin dish

Butter the casserole or gratin dish well. To plump the prunes and apricots, place them in a medium-sized saucepan with the wine or tea and cinnamon. Cover and simmer until the fruit is very tender and has absorbed most of the liquid, about 15 to 20 minutes. Soak the bread briefly in the milk, then add it to the pan, off heat, along with the rest of the ingredients except the almonds. Turn the mixture into the prepared dish and bake in a 375°F (190°C) oven for 15 minutes. Sprinkle on the sliced almonds and continue baking for another 15 minutes, or until the pudding has firmed up and the almonds are nicely browned.

Allow to cool slightly before serving. This dessert is delicious warm or cold; I must say that I prefer it warm, and it will, of course, reheat beautifully when set for 10 to 15 minutes in a moderate oven.

Un souper devant la télé

A TV DINNER FOR 6

✕

La pizza Jeannette
PIZZA WITH ONIONS, TOMATOES,
CHEESE, AND BLACK OLIVES

Blettes panachées au fromage
LAYERS OF SWISS CHARD
WITH CHEESE

Capuccino Chantilly au chocolat
COFFEE-CREAM DESSERT
WITH CHOCOLATE

*rosé du Rhône—Tavel/Rutherford Hill
Pinot Noir Blanc*

Un souper devant la télé

Americans may be surprised to learn that the French watch television during meals. But my husband Jean and I often do in the evenings, and *la pizza Jeannette* makes an easy meal to serve while everyone sits and enjoys a favorite show.

This pizza dish—really a rectangular vegetable tart, and very different from what you find in the States—is named for my precious Provençale cook Jeannette, who has cooked lovely simple food in my house for twenty years. She knows many things, my Jeannette; we have learned a lot together, and this pizza has her touch.

The *pâte à croustade* used here makes a more delectable pizza than the traditional kind made with bread dough, found in the south of France. The treatment of the onions for the filling is very important, for they must be tender and sweet and require slow and careful cooking. For the tomato sauce, the improvised version with tomato paste, which I suggest throughout this book, is *certainly* superior to a sauce made from scratch with highly acid tomatoes. If you do have good, sweet tomatoes, then by all means use them for a more conventional homemade sauce (you will find one described in *Simca's Cuisine*). You will be surprised, though, at the delicious result of refining a canned paste.

In France it is unusual to find the two parts of Swiss chard—the stalks and the leaves—served together at the same time. But for the *blettes panachées* the two are spread in separate layers in a buttered dish and lightly topped with cheese. The stalks prepared this way are quite tender and a nice contrast to the green of the leaves.

The dessert, the *capuccino Chantilly,* is nothing more than a coffee-

and chocolate-flavored custard with whipped cream folded in. It will therefore not set into a fluffy texture, as for a mousse, but will remain creamy, rather like a mayonnaise. It is certainly a dessert for those like my husband Jean, who describes it approvingly as "chocolatesque."

This TV dinner is one that can be completely done in advance and then reheated. In fact, both the pizza and the *gratin* will be almost better when rewarmed. The chocolate cream can easily wait a day in the refrigerator.

La pizza Jeannette

PIZZA WITH ONIONS, TOMATOES,
CHEESE, AND NIÇOISE OLIVES

For 6:

1 recipe *pâte à croustade*, page 211

¼ cup (½ dL) olive oil

2 pounds (900 g) onions, peeled and sliced

1 teaspoon salt

Freshly ground pepper

½ cup (45 g) each of grated Gruyère and Parmesan cheese, mixed together

⅔ cup (1½ dL) quick tomato sauce, page 220

1 ounce (30 g) tiny black *niçoise* olives, pitted and halved or quartered, depending on size

Recommended equipment: A 4-quart (4 L) heavy-bottomed saucepan or skillet with a lid

Make the dough and allow it to chill while you prepare the onions.

Heat the oil in the saucepan or skillet, add the onions, and stir them for a minute or two over medium heat to coat them with the oil. Cover the pan and lower the heat; cook the onions for 15 to 20 minutes, stirring them from time to time, until they are beginning to be tender.

Uncover the pan and continue cooking and stirring occasionally until the onions are very tender and sweet—for about 20 to 30 minutes more. Season and place in a fine sieve lined with a paper towel to drain.

Roll out the pastry to a rectangle 10 x 16 inches (25 x 40 cm) and about ⅛ inch (⅓ cm) thick. Place on a baking sheet and pinch up the sides, pressing the corners firmly together, to make a nice standing edge about ¾ inch (2 cm) high. Sprinkle a bit of the cheese over the dough, and chill in the freezer for 10 or 15 minutes.

Remove from the freezer. Spread the onions in an even layer along the bottom and sprinkle on a bit more cheese. Pour the tomato sauce over the onions and spread evenly. Sprinkle on the remaining cheese and top with the olives in a nice design. Bake in a 400°F (205°C) oven for 25 to 30 minutes, until the cheese is lightly browned and the pastry is done. Remove to room temperature and allow to cool for at least 20 minutes before serving.

This dish is good eaten warm or cold, and can be reheated in a 350°F (180°C) oven for 10 to 15 minutes. To serve, slice the pizza down the center, then cut rectangular slices from each side.

Blettes panachées au fromage
LAYERS OF SWISS CHARD WITH CHEESE

For 6:

3 pounds (1350 g) fresh Swiss
   chard
6 tablespoons (85 g) butter
2 cloves garlic, peeled and
   minced
1½ teaspoons salt
Freshly ground pepper

¼ cup (½ dL) cream
3 tablespoons all-purpose flour
2 cups (½ L) milk
Freshly grated nutmeg
½ cup (45 g) grated Gruyère
   cheese

Recommended equipment: A large oval gratin dish

Butter the gratin dish well. Cut off the leafy part of the chard, wash, and drain. Trim away any bruised bits from the stems and peel them to remove all of the stringy surface. Slice the stems into strips about 1 inch (2½ cm) long and ¼ inch (⅔ cm) wide.

Cook the greens in a large quantity of rapidly boiling salted water for 3 to 4 minutes, until they are just tender. Remove with a skimmer, refresh in cold water, and set aside to drain thoroughly. Add the chard stems to the boiling water and cook until they are tender, for 5 to 8 minutes. Drain and set aside.

Place the greens in a strong kitchen towel and squeeze out the excess moisture. Chop roughly in a food processor or with a knife. In a skillet melt 2 tablespoons (30 g) butter, add the garlic, and cook gently for 1 minute. Add the chopped greens and sauté for 2 to 3 minutes over medium heat, to evaporate the last of the moisture. Stir in 1 teaspoon salt, pepper, and the cream. Taste for seasoning.

Melt 2 tablespoons (30 g) butter in a small saucepan set over medium heat, stir in the flour, and cook for a minute or two. Whisk in the milk all at once and bring the sauce to a simmer, stirring until thickened and smooth. Add ½ teaspoon salt, pepper, and nutmeg. Taste for seasoning. Mix the chard stems with the sauce. Spread half of the stems in the bottom of the prepared gratin dish, add the chopped greens in a single layer, and top with the remaining stems. Sprinkle with the cheese and dot with the remaining butter. The dish may now wait for 1 or 2 hours at room temperature before baking.

Bake in a 400°F (205°C) oven for 15 to 20 minutes, until the cheese is beginning to brown lightly; if you wish, run the dish for a few seconds under a hot broiler to help it brown. Allow to cool a few minutes before serving. If allowed to cool completely, the dish should be reheated in a hot oven for 12 to 15 minutes.

Capuccino Chantilly au chocolat

COFFEE-CREAM DESSERT WITH CHOCOLATE

For 6:

½ pound (225 g) semisweet chocolate, broken into bits
⅔ cup (1½ dL) evaporated milk
2 tablespoons instant coffee granules

Pinch of salt
3 egg yolks
1 cup (¼ L) heavy cream
2 teaspoons vanilla extract
¼ cup (30 g) powdered sugar

Recommended equipment: A 1-quart (1 L) serving bowl

Place the chocolate, milk, coffee, and pinch of salt in a heavy-bottomed saucepan and set over low heat, stirring occasionally until the chocolate has melted and the mixture is smooth. Off heat stir in the egg yolks, then return the pan to medium heat for about 1 minute, stirring constantly, to warm the yolks and thicken the chocolate. Pour the mixture into a metal mixing bowl and stir over ice water until it is cold.

Beat the cream with the vanilla and powdered sugar until it is stiff. If you wish, reserve a small amount for decorating the dessert, then fold the rest into the cooled chocolate mixture. Pour into the serving bowl and chill for at least 1 hour before serving.

Garnish with the reserved *Chantilly* piped through a pastry bag equipped with a star tip, or simply sift on a dusting of powdered sugar mixed, perhaps, with unsweetened cocoa. Spoon the dessert onto plates.

Menus with Fish and Shellfish

MAIN DISHES:

Filets de poisson étouffés sur l'assiette

Ruche de poisson à l'oseille

Crabes farcis gratinés

Couronne de soles aux épinards

Les chaudrées pitchounes

Un déjeuner en rêvant des îles

A LUNCH FOR 4, DREAMING OF
THE SOUTH SEAS

Ramequins au fromage
INDIVIDUAL CHEESE CUSTARDS

Filets de poisson étouffés sur l'assiette
FISH FILLETS WITH FRESH HERBS,
STEAMED ON INDIVIDUAL PLATES

Concombres au beurre
CUCUMBERS IN BUTTER

Les fausses frites de Bramafam
OVEN POTATOES WITH A LITTLE GARLIC

La Hawaiienne
MACADAMIA NUT CAKE WITH
RUM-FLAVORED BUTTER CREAM

*vin blanc fruité—Sancerre/Sterling Vineyards
Sauvignon Blanc*

Un déjeuner en rêvant des îles

A LUNCH FOR 4, DREAMING OF
THE SOUTH SEAS

My recent discovery of the lovely Hawaiian Islands is a time I will never forget, and I often dream of returning there. This lunch of the freshest fish seems to bring that moment a little closer. The main course is steamed right on the plate in which it is served, making it a light and easy dish that keeps all the flavor of the fish. This is, however, a preparation best done for a very few; should you wish to serve a larger group, I have given special instructions at the end of the recipe. Use any good fresh fish for this dish. At home in France, I would use fillets of fresh Dover sole, or a whole boned trout. In Hawaii it would be mahi-mahi, I suppose. And for those who live between those two places, there are many good possibilities, which are given in the recipe.

To go with the dish are *les fausses frites de Bramafam,* an excellent potato dish for any informal preparation of fish, roasted meat, or fowl. It is uncomplicated—the potatoes are first boiled, then finished in the oven with butter—and with the use of a French-fry cutting device, the preparation is very rapid and attractive at the same time.

I must say that the splendid stretches of the South Pacific brought fresh air to many of my cooking ideas. The dessert in this menu, *La Hawaiienne,* is a cake made with macadamia nuts, for which my admiration is complete. Who knows, one day the macadamia may be popular in Provence, as I now have growing in my window a little macadamia tree carried back from Hawaii, which will produce, I am told, one nut at the end of seven years! In the meantime this nut is virtually unknown in France—even in the United States it is a little expensive—so you could substitute almonds, if you wish. But the macadamia is so delicate in flavor, and so very rich, that I feel it is really preferable here; when pulverized, it is beautiful and smooth, and becomes the base for the batter as well as for the butter cream.

Ramequins au fromage
INDIVIDUAL CHEESE CUSTARDS

For 4 to 6:

4 eggs
2 tablespoons all-purpose flour
1 cup (¼ L) heavy cream, or
    half milk and half cream
Freshly ground pepper

Freshly grated nutmeg
¼ teaspoon salt
1 cup (90 g) grated Gruyère
    and Parmesan cheese, mixed

Recommended equipment: Six ½-cup (1 dL) porcelain ramequins

Butter the ramequins well. Separate two of the eggs.

Place the flour in a medium-sized saucepan. Whisk in the cream (or cream and milk) by drops to make a thick paste, and then in a steady stream as the flour smooths out; don't worry if the sauce has a few lumps (it will even out later). Beat in the 2 whole eggs plus the 2 yolks and set the pan over medium heat, whisking until the mixture comes to a simmer and thickens to a smooth sauce. (The eggs cannot scramble, as they are supported by the flour.) Off heat add the seasonings and set the sauce aside.

Beat the egg whites with a pinch of salt until they form stiff peaks. Fold the cheese, along with the warm sauce, into the beaten whites and turn the mixture into the prepared molds. These can wait for up to an hour at room temperature before baking in a 375°F (190°C) oven for 15 to 18 minutes. They will puff nicely and be lightly browned. Serve at once. They are really at their best when freshly baked.

Filets de poisson étouffés sur l'assiette

FISH FILLETS WITH FRESH HERBS, STEAMED
ON INDIVIDUAL PLATES

For 4:

1½ pounds (675 g) boneless fish
fillets—sole, lake whitefish,
red snapper, sea bass, etc.
8 tablespoons (115 g) butter, at
room temperature
1 teaspoon salt

Freshly ground pepper
4 teaspoons lemon juice
2 tablespoons chopped fresh
herbs—tarragon, thyme and
parsley, or dill—or 1 teaspoon
dried tarragon

Recommended equipment: 4 large porcelain dinner plates

Trim the fish fillets into 8 serving pieces, about ¼ inch (⅔ cm) thick;
if necessary, flatten with the broad side of a cleaver or a heavy knife.
Smear half of the butter onto the center of the plates, arrange two
pieces of fish on each, and sprinkle with the seasonings, lemon juice,
and herbs. Dot with the remaining butter. Wrap each plate with a
piece of foil, tucking the edges under snugly. The garnished plates
are now ready to steam, or you may refrigerate them for several hours.
Remove to room temperature 1 hour before cooking.

To steam the fish, bring about 1 inch (2½ cm) of water to a boil
in two medium-sized saucepans, then set a prepared plate over each
of the pans. Cook over the boiling water for 5 to 8 minutes; the time
will depend on the type of fish as well as the thickness of the plate.
To test, lift a corner of the foil; the fillets are done when they just
begin to flake apart when pricked with a fork; they should not be dry.
When the first two plates are done, set them aside while you finish
the others. Set all four plates in a 350°F (180 C°) oven for 2 to 4 minutes just before serving to rewarm them and cook the top of the fish.
Remove the foil at the table to allow each person a burst of fragrant
steam.

Variation: Filets de poisson étouffés au four (Fish fillets baked in the oven). If you want to serve a larger group, it is best to do this dish in the oven. For 8 servings, double the ingredients and wrap each serving tightly inside pieces of buttered foil. (No plates are used here.) Arrange on a baking sheet and bake at 400°F (205°C) for 6 to 10 minutes, until the fish is done, as described above. Serve in the foil set on individual plates.

Variation II: Truites à l'étouffées (Steamed trout). A very succulent dish can be made with whole fresh trout that are split open down the back and all the meat peeled back to remove the backbone. The fish is then seasoned as in the master recipe, and laid butterfly fashion (skin side up) on the plate and steamed as directed.

Concombres au beurre

CUCUMBERS IN BUTTER

For 6:

2 pounds (900 g) cucumbers
4 tablespoons (60 g) butter
⅔ cup (1½ dL) water
1½ teaspoons salt

Freshly ground pepper
Chopped fresh parsley, tarragon, or dill

Recommended equipment: A melon ball cutter

Peel the cucumbers, slice them in half lengthwise, and scrape out their seeds with a spoon. Cut out attractive balls of cucumber; save any trimmings for a soup or a salad.

Melt the butter in a medium-sized saucepan, then add the cucumbers, water, and seasonings and cook, partially covered, over medium-low heat until the cucumber is nearly tender, for about 10 to 15 minutes. Remove the lid and continue simmering until nearly all of the liquid has evaporated and the cucumbers are glazing in the butter. Sprinkle on the chopped herbs, correct the seasoning, and turn the cucumbers into a hot vegetable dish.

To cook the cucumbers an hour or two ahead of time, prepare them as directed and remove them from the heat after they have glazed. When ready to serve, rewarm them and sprinkle with the green herbs.

Les fausses frites de Bramafam

OVEN POTATOES WITH A LITTLE GARLIC

For 6:

1½ pounds (675 g) boiling
   potatoes, peeled
5 tablespoons (70 g) butter
1½ teaspoons salt
Freshly ground pepper

Fresh grated nutmeg
1 clove garlic, peeled and
   minced
1 tablespoon finely chopped
   parsley

Recommended equipment: A food processor equipped with the French-fry disk; a medium-sized gratin dish

Using a food processor or working with a knife, cut the potatoes into medium-sized French-fry shapes—about 2 inches (5 cm) long and ¼ inch (¾ cm) thick. Cook for 5 minutes in boiling salted water. Drain and refresh in cold water, then drain again thoroughly, and pat dry in a towel. Butter a baking dish heavily, and in it arrange layers of the potatoes, seasoning each layer as you go. Dot with the butter and sprinkle on the garlic. The dish may now wait for an hour or two before baking.

Bake in a 425°F (220°C) oven for 15 to 20 minutes, until the potatoes are very tender, stirring gently once or twice to coat evenly with the butter. Serve sprinkled with the parsley.

La Hawaiienne

MACADAMIA NUT CAKE WITH
RUM-FLAVORED BUTTER CREAM

For a 9-inch (23 cm) cake serving 6 to 8:

For the cake:

½ cup (65 g) all-purpose flour
½ teaspoon baking powder
8 ounces (230 g) unsalted
  macadamia nuts (see page 14)
⅓ cup (100 g) plus 2
  tablespoons granulated sugar

4 tablespoons (60 g) unsalted
  butter, at room temperature
4 eggs, separated
Pinch of salt

For the butter cream:

6 tablespoons (85 g) unsalted
  butter
1 cup (115 g) powdered sugar

4 tablespoons dark rum
7 or 8 pistachios, blanched,
  peeled and roughly chopped

Recommended equipment: A food processor equipped with the metal blade; a 9-inch (23 cm) cake pan

Place a piece of buttered waxed paper in the bottom of the pan, then butter the sides generously. Toast the nuts in a 350°F (180°C) oven for 8 to 10 minutes, until golden brown, then allow to cool slightly. Sift the flour with the baking powder.

Pulverize 4 ounces (115 g) of the macadamia nuts in the food processor with 2 tablespoons of sugar until they are very fine; this will take about 1 minute. Then beat in the butter and egg yolks, mixing until smooth.

In a separate bowl, beat the egg whites with the pinch of salt until they form soft peaks. Sprinkle on the remaining granulated sugar and

45

continue beating until the meringue holds fairly stiff peaks. Beat one-third of the whites into the macadamia mixture to lighten it, then beat in the flour. Fold the mixture into the remaining whites until well blended. Turn the batter into the prepared pan. Bake in a 375°F (190°C) oven for 20 to 25 minutes, until the cake has risen nicely, has pulled away from the sides of the pan, and is slightly golden. Remove the pan to a cooling rack. After 10 minutes run a knife or spatula around the inside edges and unmold the cake onto a serving dish; remove the waxed paper.

While the cake cools completely, make the butter cream: pulverize the remaining macadamia nuts in a food processor, then beat in the butter, powdered sugar, and 2 tablespoons of the rum. Turn into a small bowl; if the butter cream is very soft, set it in the refrigerator for a few minutes to firm up.

Using a serrated knife, slice the cake in half to make two even layers. Sprinkle the remaining rum over the cut surfaces of the cake to make them moist, then spread one layer with about one-third of the butter cream. Place the second layer firmly on top, and spread the remaining butter cream smoothly over the top and sides of the cake. Sprinkle the chopped pistachios around the edges. The *Hawaiienne* will store well for a day or two in the refrigerator. Remove it to room temperature 30 minutes before serving so that the macadamia butter will be creamy.

Un déjeuner de bienvenue

A WELCOMING LUNCH FOR 6

Crème de concombres
COLD CUCUMBER SOUP WITH
TOMATO GARNISH

Ruche de poisson à l'oseille
SIMCA'S BEEHIVE FISH PÂTÉ
WITH SORREL

Asperges au beurre
FRESH BUTTERED ASPARAGUS

Irish coffee soufflé

*Côtes de Provence rosé—Bandol Coeur
de Grain/Caymus "Oeil de Perdrix"*

Un déjeuner de bienvenue

A WELCOMING LUNCH FOR 6

Something that has always struck me in the United States is the warmth extended to newcomers. There is a good deal more of this spirit than we have in France, where one does not always make friends immediately. After many trips to America, I must say I have been taught a little about welcoming strangers myself. And this menu, with an amusing fish pâté molded in macaroni to resemble a beehive, is the sort of gay meal I would serve to make people feel at home.

The cold soup of cucumber is perhaps a familiar first course, especially agreeable for warm weather. But Michael and I have given it a different treatment here, with a light base of potato for body and flavor. The soup, then, needs only a light enrichment of sour cream, so it is not overly rich, a criticism I often have of cold soups. The garnish of chopped cucumber and tomato adds a further refreshing touch. If, by the way, you can find the kind of unwaxed cucumbers that in America are often called "English," the soup can be made with the cucumbers left unpeeled, which will give a cool hint of green. But certainly it can be made with the usual cucumbers as well, with the thicker and often bitter peel removed.

For the fish, there are really no special techniques. If you wished, you could simplify the dish by omitting the macaroni and baking the pâté in the plain well-buttered mold. But the "beehive" presentation is fun to do, and adds an interesting texture. A layer of sorrel cooked in cream garnishes the center of the *ruche,* and the accompanying cream sauce with sorrel will enhance this tart flavoring, always delicious with fish. Of course, sorrel is sometimes difficult to obtain in the United States, so you could use a mushroom flavoring instead and serve with a tomato cream sauce, as directed at the end of the recipe.

A soufflé for dessert is always a little spectacular, and gives a lively finish to any meal. The soufflé base here is a *crème patissière,* made with a mixture of flour and potato starch that I feel helps give a very light result. The coffee flavoring is inspired by that delicious and very intoxicating drink, Irish coffee. However, in a soufflé the dose of whiskey is rather more harmless.

Crème de concombres

COLD CUCUMBER SOUP WITH TOMATO GARNISH

For 6:

3 tablespoons (45 g) butter
1 large onion, peeled and sliced
1 pound (450 g) boiling
   potatoes, peeled and cut into
   1-inch (2½ cm) pieces
6 cups (1½ L) light chicken
   broth or water
Salt and freshly ground pepper

1¼ to 1½ pounds (565–675 g)
   cucumbers—preferably the
   "English" variety, unwaxed
1 large, ripe tomato, peeled,
   seeded and finely diced
1 cup (¼ L) sour cream
1 tablespoon chopped fresh
   parsley or chervil

Recommended equipment: An electric blender

Melt the butter in a 5- to 6-quart (5–6 L) pot, mix in the onion and sauté over medium-low heat, stirring occasionally, for 6 to 8 minutes. Add the potatoes, pour on the chicken broth or water, and season lightly. Bring to a boil and cook for 8 to 10 minutes, until the potatoes are nearly tender.

    Leave the cucumbers unpeeled if they are the unwaxed variety; if not, they should be peeled. Set aside ¼ pound (115 g) for a garnish. Slice the remaining cucumbers into ½-inch (1½ cm) chunks and add to the pot. Boil rapidly until tender, about 8 to 10 minutes. When done,

49

purée the soup in the blender in 2 or 3 lots. Set aside to cool, then refrigerate until cold.

Slice the reserved cucumber in half lengthwise and scoop out the seeds with a spoon. Dice fine and add to the diced tomatoes. Season lightly.

When the soup is cold, whisk in the sour cream, stir in the cucumber-tomato garnish, and correct the seasoning. Keep refrigerated until ready to serve. Sprinkle each serving with the fresh herbs.

Ruche de poisson à l'oseille

SIMCA'S BEEHIVE FISH PÂTÉ WITH SORREL

For 6 to 8:

¼ pound (115 g) macaroni at least 10 inches (25 cm) long

¼ pound (115 g) fresh sorrel, stemmed and washed, the leaves torn in half if they are large

3 tablespoons heavy cream

1¾ teaspoons salt

Freshly ground pepper

1 pound (450 g) boneless fish fillets—sole, snapper, lake whitefish, etc.

1⅓ cups (70 g) fresh white bread crumbs

½ pound (225 g) cream cheese, preferably without gum additives, or a mild goat cheese

2 teaspoons *herbes de Provence* (see page 220)

Several sprigs fresh herbs— parsley with basil or chives

Pinch of cayenne

3 eggs

Sorrel Sauce (see below)

Recommended equipment: A 1½-quart (1½ L) plain metal mold— stainless mixing bowl, charlotte mold, etc.; a food processor equipped with the metal blade; and a food mill

Cook the macaroni slightly past the *al dente* stage in boiling salted water, or about 6 to 8 minutes; the macaroni must be supple enough to line the mold easily. Drain in a colander, refresh briefly under cold running water, then set aside to drain thoroughly.

Butter the mold generously. Line the mold with the macaroni—it should be very dry and a little sticky, which will help it hold—in a single-layered spiral, beginning at the bottom edge of the mold, working in to the center; then work up the sides. For the very center, you will need to poke in short, stray pieces of macaroni to fill the gaps; don't worry if it is not perfect. Set in the refrigerator.

Place a medium-sized skillet (preferably nonstick) over high heat and add the sorrel to it a few leaves at a time, stirring constantly until all the sorrel is wilted. Lower the heat, pour on the cream, and simmer for 2 to 3 minutes, until the sorrel is very tender and has thickened nicely with the cream. Season with ¼ teaspoon salt and some pepper; set aside.

Purée the fish in the food processor, and to make the finest purée put it through the medium disk of the food mill to remove any stringy bits of skin and bone. Turn into a bowl. In the processor beat together the bread crumbs, cream cheese, herbs, remaining salt and pepper, the cayenne, and the eggs. Stir into the purée and taste the mixture carefully for seasoning. (If you are working by hand, cut the fish into small pieces, then put it through the medium disk of the food mill. Beat the cream cheese with the eggs, then add the bread crumbs,

dried and fresh herbs [chopped]. Combine the fish purée with the cheese mixture, add the salt, pepper, and cayenne, and taste carefully for seasoning.)

Carefully press a layer of the mixture into the bottom of the mold, to hold the macaroni in place. Then fill the mold with one-half of the fish mixture, packing it firmly against the sides. Stir 3 or 4 tablespoons of the fish mixture into the sorrel to give it some body, then spread on in an even layer. Fill the mold with the remaining fish mixture, remove any extra macaroni from the sides, and knock the bowl sharply two or three times on a flat surface to help settle the pâté. Cover with a piece of buttered waxed paper or foil. Once filled, the mold can wait in the refrigerator for several hours, or overnight, before it is baked. One and one-half hours before it goes in the oven, remove to room temperature.

Bake in a *bain-marie*—with simmering water ⅓ of the way up its sides—in a 375°F (190°C) oven for 35 to 40 minutes, until a knife inserted in the center comes out clean. Allow to rest for 15 to 20 minutes at room temperature before unmolding onto a serving platter. Drain off into the sauce any juices that accumulate.

Cut the "beehive" into wedges with a very sharp knife, and serve with a spoonful or two of hot sorrel cream sauce. Pass any remaining sauce in a sauceboat. The pâté can also be served cold, when it would be good with the *nouvelle sauce verte* on page 217.

Sauce crème à l'oseille
SORREL CREAM SAUCE

For 1⅓ cups (3¼ dL):

2 cups (½ L) heavy cream	1 teaspoon salt
¼ pound (115 g) sorrel, stemmed and washed, the leaves torn in half if large	Freshly ground pepper

Simmer the cream in a heavy-bottomed saucepan over medium-low heat for 10 to 15 minutes, until it has reduced by about one-third and has thickened slightly. Stir in the sorrel and allow it to wilt in the sauce for 1 or 2 minutes over heat. Add the salt and pepper, tasting carefully for seasoning.

The sauce can wait for an hour at room temperature; stir over gentle heat to rewarm.

Variation: Ruche de poisson aux champignons (Fish pâté with mushrooms). If sorrel is unavailable, you could make an attractive *ruche* by substituting half the recipe for creamy minced mushrooms on page 219. In this case, I would recommend the quick tomato sauce on page 220, enriched with a little cream, as a nice accompaniment.

Irish coffee soufflé

For 6:

1⅓ cups (3¼ dL) milk
2 tablespoons instant coffee
   granules
1 teaspoon vanilla extract
½ cup (100 g) plus 2
   tablespoons granulated sugar
6 eggs, separated

2 tablespoons all-purpose flour
2 tablespoons potato starch
4 to 5 tablespoons Irish whiskey
Pinch of salt
¼ teaspoon cream of tartar
   (optional)
Powdered sugar, in a shaker

Recommended equipment: An 8-cup (2 L) porcelain soufflé mold

Butter and lightly sugar the inside of the mold. In a medium-sized saucepan, bring the milk to a simmer over low heat with the coffee and vanilla. While the milk is warming, whisk the ½ cup sugar gradually into the egg yolks, beating them until they are thick and "make a ribbon," 1 or 2 minutes. Beat in the flour and potato starch. Whisk in the hot milk, pouring in a slow stream and then more rapidly. Return the mixture to the saucepan, then whisk it over medium-high heat until it comes to a boil and thickens to a smooth cream. Remove from the heat and stir in the whiskey.

The soufflé base may now wait at room temperature for an hour or two with a piece of plastic wrap pressed directly on its surface. Before proceeding with the recipe, stir the *crème patissière* over medium-low heat until it is hot to the finger.

Beat the egg whites with the pinch of salt until they form soft peaks (if you are using a stainless mixing bowl, add ¼ teaspoon cream of tartar to the whites when you begin beating them). Add the 2 table-spoons sugar and continue beating until stiff. Delicately fold in the hot sauce. Pour the soufflé mixture into the prepared mold and bake in a 400°F (205°C) oven for 18 to 22 minutes, depending on how soft you prefer the center. The soufflé should rise 2 or 3 inches (5 to 8 cm) above the rim of the mold. Sprinkle the surface with powdered sugar and serve at once, spooned onto plates.

Un menu sur la Côte

A MENU FOR 6 DURING CRAB SEASON

Ratatouille en estouffade
EGGPLANT, ZUCCHINI, AND BELL
PEPPERS BAKED WITH RICE

Crabes farcis gratinés
GRATINÉED FRESH CRABS

Glace à la banane, sauce au chocolat
BANANA ICE CREAM WITH
CHOCOLATE SAUCE

*Côtes du Rhône rouge —
Bandol/Stag's Leap Zinfandel*

Un menu sur la Côte

A MENU FOR 6 DURING CRAB SEASON

Freshly caught crab is one of the most delicious things to eat, whether they are the large French *tourteaux,* or the American Dungeness found on the West Coast. Of course, eating them simply boiled in a good court bouillon and served warm with a lemon butter, or cold with a creamy mayonnaise, is what any lover of fresh crab will prefer, as nothing can interfere with the delicate, sweet taste. But there is something to be said for a richly flavored stuffed crab as well, that can be prepared in advance and reheated.

The first course in this menu is a variation on the *ratatouille* so familiar in Provençal cooking. Here the sautéing of the vegetables is rather simplified, and when the dish is put to bake, a little partially cooked rice is added to help absorb all the savory juices. When completely cooked, the vegetables in the *estouffade* will be very tender, almost a compote, and the flavors very rich. There is no point here in having *al dente* vegetables; in fact I often find this idea carried too far. Many green vegetables are very good left with a *slightly* crisp texture, but they should be properly cooked, never *raw!* This I deplore. But in any case, in this very rustic dish there is no question of that, and you should allow the full cooking time.

For the *crabes farcis gratinés,* I use a well-flavored purée of stewed leeks, bound with bread soaked in cream, to mix with the cooked crab meat, which is then piled in the shells and reheated at the last moment. It is a complete course in itself, to be followed only by salad, and perhaps some cheese, before the dessert. While the dish is ideal for people living on the coast, where the season for fresh crab is generous, my inland readers certainly could use frozen crab or fresh lump crab meat, in which case the dish could be prepared in individual ramekins.

As for the banana ice cream with chocolate, it is not terribly rich, as ice creams go, and it is simple to make. The banana purée is mixed with beaten cream and egg white, layered with chocolate, and then set to freeze for 4 to 5 hours. If you wish to hurry things up, you can make the dessert in a regular ice-cream maker omitting the chocolate garnish and then serve it scooped into bowls and topped with the sauce.

Ratatouille en estouffade

EGGPLANT, ZUCCHINI, AND BELL PEPPERS BAKED WITH RICE

For 8 to 10:

½ cup (100 g) long-grain white rice
½ cup (1 dL) olive oil
5 cloves garlic, peeled and minced
1 pound (450 g) onions, peeled and sliced
1 pound (450 g) eggplant, peeled and cut into ½-inch (1¼ cm) cubes
1 pound (450 g) zucchini, trimmed, washed, and sliced into rounds ⅛ inch (⅓ cm) thick
1 pound (450 g) red or green bell peppers, seeded and cut into strips

3 pounds (1350 g) fresh tomatoes, peeled, seeded, and chopped, or 2 cans, 35 ounces (1000 g) each, Italian-style plum tomatoes, drained, seeded, and chopped
3 tablespoons chopped fresh parsley and basil, mixed
2½ teaspoons salt
Freshly ground pepper
½ cup (1 dL) chicken broth
½ cup (45 g) grated cheese— Gruyère and Parmesan, mixed (optional)
A few drops of olive oil (optional)

Recommended equipment: A 6- to 8-quart (6–8 L) ovenproof casserole with a lid

Stir the rice into 2 quarts (2 L) boiling salted water and cook it for 8 minutes. Drain and refresh under cold running water. Set aside to drain thoroughly.

Heat the oil in the casserole, add the garlic and onions, and gently sauté over medium-low heat for 6 to 8 minutes, stirring occasionally, until the onions are beginning to be tender. Stir in the eggplant. After 2 minutes toss in the zucchini and cook for 20 minutes, stirring frequently. Remove two-thirds of the vegetables from the pan. Spread the remaining vegetables in a layer, and add alternating layers of the red or green peppers, tomatoes, rice, and the cooked vegetables until all of the ingredients are used up. Sprinkle with a bit of the herbs and season each layer as you go. Pour in the chicken broth, cover, and bake in a 350°F (180°C) oven for 1 hour: the vegetables should be very tender, but not a purée.

The *ratatouille* is delicious made the day before and then reheated. (There is plenty here for leftovers, very good cold.) It can be served from the casserole or from a serving platter, or if you wish to gratiné it, turn into a large oval gratin dish, sprinkle with the cheese, drizzle the olive oil over it and bake in a 400°F (205°C) oven for 15 to 20 minutes, until hot through. Then run under a broiler until the cheese is bubbling and brown.

�

Crabes farcis gratinés

GRATINÉED FRESH CRABS

For 6:

6 fresh-cooked crabs, about
   1 pound (450 g) each, or 1½
   pounds (675 g) lump crab
   meat
4 ounces (115 g) fresh bread,
   without the crust
1 cup (¼ L) heavy cream
4 medium-sized shallots, peeled
2 cloves garlic, peeled
5 or 6 large sprigs of parsley

½ pound (225 g) fresh leeks
6 tablespoons (85 g) butter
2 hard-boiled eggs, peeled
Juice of 1 lemon
1 teaspoon *herbes de Provence*
   (see page 220)
1½ teaspoons salt
Freshly ground pepper
¼ cup (30 g) stale bread crumbs

Recommended equipment: If you are using lump crab meat—6 individual ovenproof dishes of about 1 cup (¼ L) capacity

Remove the crab backs in one piece, scrape out the soft brown "butter" into a bowl, and set the shells aside. Remove all of the white meat from the body, the legs, and claws, and add to the bowl, being sure to discard the little gray fins and any blackish bits. (If you are using lump crab meat, pick through it to remove any possible bits of shell.) Refrigerate the crab until you are ready to use it.

    Cut the bread into cubes and set it to soak in the cream. Make a *persillade* by chopping the shallots, garlic, and parsley in a food processor or with a knife. Trim and wash the leeks carefully, removing the roots and any of the tough or dirty green. Chop the leeks coarsely and cook in 4 tablespoons (60 g) of the butter, covered and over low heat, for 8 to 10 minutes, stirring occasionally. Uncover, add the *persillade,* and continue cooking until the leeks are tender, or another 4 or 5 minutes. Purée in the food processor with the bread and cream and the hard boiled eggs, or put through the medium disk

59

of a food mill. Turn the mixture into a mixing bowl and stir in the crab, lemon juice, seasonings, and herbs.

Divide the stuffing equally among the crab shells or mound it neatly into well-buttered individual dishes. Sprinkle on the bread crumbs and dot with the remaining 2 tablespoons (30 g) butter. This may now wait at room temperature for up to one hour, or be refrigerated for several hours, in which case remove to room temperature 45 minutes before serving. To finish, place the shells or the dishes on a baking sheet and bake in a 450°F (230°C) oven for 15 to 20 minutes. Serve at once.

Glace à la banane, sauce au chocolat

BANANA ICE CREAM WITH CHOCOLATE SAUCE

For 1 quart (1 L) ice cream, serving 6:

6 ounces (170 g) semisweet
   chocolate, broken into bits
5 tablespoons dark rum
½ cup (1 dL) unsweetened
   evaporated milk
1¼ pounds (565 g) ripe bananas

Grated zest and juice of 1 lime
½ cup (100 g) sugar
1 egg white
Pinch of salt
⅔ cup (1½ dL) heavy cream
½ teaspoon vanilla extract

Recommended equipment: A 1-quart (1 L) square ice-cream mold (or any other similar metal mold)

In a saucepan, melt the chocolate with 3 tablespoons of the rum over low heat, stirring occasionally until smooth. Off heat stir in the evaporated milk. Set aside to cool.

Peel the bananas and purée them in a food processor or a food mill. Add the zest and juice of the lime, the remaining rum, and ¼ cup (50 g) of the sugar. Beat the mixture until it is well blended and fluffy. Beat the egg white with the pinch of salt until it forms soft peaks. Sprinkle on the other ¼ cup (50 g) sugar and continue beating until the meringue forms fairly stiff peaks. Whip the cream until it is stiff. Combine the meringue with the whipped cream, then fold in the banana purée. Fill the mold with half of the banana mixture, spoon in half of the melted chocolate mixture in an even layer—reserving the rest for the sauce—and finish filling the mold with the remaining banana purée. Set the mold in the freezer for at least 4 to 5 hours before serving. It can be made a day ahead and frozen, but the dessert will really be at its best if served with a slightly soft center.

To serve, run a flexible metal spatula around the edges of the mold and, if it seems necessary, briefly dip the bottom in warm water, then pat dry and invert onto a serving dish. Serve the dessert cut in wedges; pass the chocolate sauce, briefly rewarmed and thinned with extra drops of rum, or even water, if it is too thick.

Un menu coloré d'été

A COLORFUL SUMMER MENU FOR 8

Les oeufs niçois
PROVENÇAL SCRAMBLED EGGS
IN TOMATOES

Couronne de soles aux épinards,
sauce beurre blanc
TURBAN OF SOLE WITH SPINACH
AND WHITE BUTTER SAUCE

Pommes vapeur
STEAMED POTATOES

Tartes jumelles aux fruits tricolores
TWIN RED-WHITE-AND-BLUE RASPBERRY
AND BLUEBERRY TARTS

Riesling d'Alsace / Robert Mondavi
Johannisberg Riesling

Un menu coloré d'été

In this breezy lunch for a fine summer day, *les oeufs niçois* are a colorful first course of creamy, gently scrambled eggs flavored with fresh basil, spooned into hollowed-out tomatoes, and served tepid. Certainly, if you wanted to prepare this dish out of tomato season, you could simply serve the eggs in little ramequins. The fresh basil flavoring in that case would easily change to fresh tarragon, or some other fresh herb. But wonderful tomatoes make it quite a special dish, and it is well worth waiting for the first juicy crop of the summer.

The *couronne* of sole is a pleasing dish in which the fish mousse, bright with fresh spinach, contrasts with the sole fillets to make a pretty ring of green and white. A creamy white butter sauce (*beurre blanc*) is very good here, but you could also serve a *velouté,* made with a concentrated stock and finished with cream and egg yolks, or a rich hollandaise. Also, on a quite warm day the dish could very nicely be served cold, along with the *sauce mousseline* on page 219. By the way, this fish mousse contains only ⅓ cup (¾ dL) of cream. I feel that it is not always necessary to enrich a fish mousse heavily with cream; also, in this dish the mixture is lightened with cream cheese, besides the usual eggs.

The twin *tartes aux fruits tricolores* are really two separate tarts— one raspberry and one blueberry—that are sliced and reassembled with alternating glazed and sugared slices, creating an elegant effect of red-white-and-blue that is fun for a Fourth, or Fourteenth, of July. The blueberries, which tend to be very tart, I like baked in the pastry with some sugar; on the other hand the raspberries, which should be very sweet and ripe, go into a fully baked tart shell with a little *Chantilly* and then some red-currant glaze to make them shine. This is a dessert for berries in their prime, and their simple preparation in delicate pastry makes a most refreshing end to a summer meal. During other months, you could vary the fruit: in winter, for example, the tarts could be done with sautéed apples, baked in the shells and then arranged with alternating glazed and sugared slices.

❦

Les oeufs niçois

PROVENÇAL SCRAMBLED EGGS
IN TOMATOES

For 8:

8 firm, ripe tomatoes
Salt and freshly ground pepper
8 large cloves garlic, peeled
24 fresh basil leaves (in season)
1 teaspoon *herbes de Provence*
   (see page 220)
10 eggs
5 tablespoons olive oil

1 hard-boiled egg, peeled and
   sliced
1 tablespoon capers
4 anchovy fillets, sliced in half
   lengthwise
8 clean, crisp lettuce leaves
24 cherry tomatoes

Recommended equipment: An 11- to 12-inch (30 cm) nonstick skillet; a mortar and pestle

Cut a slice about ¼ inch (⅔ cm) thick off the top of each tomato, then seed the tomatoes by squeezing them gently over a bowl and working your finger around inside. Strain out the seeds and save the juice. Scoop out the pulp (being sure not to scrape the sides), using a small spoon, and chop it roughly. Salt and pepper the inside of the tomatoes and set them aside.

Add the reserved tomato juice to the skillet, along with the chopped tomato, and cook the mixture, uncovered, over medium-low heat for 12 to 15 minutes, stirring occasionally, until it has thickened into a nice paste. Season with ½ teaspoon salt and a little pepper, and transfer to a bowl. Blanch the garlic for 6 minutes in boiling water to cover. Drain and chop finely with 16 of the fresh basil leaves, using the flat side of the knife to press the mixture into a purée. Add the garlic and herb paste to the concentrated tomato, along with the *herbes de Provence*.

Heat the oil in the same skillet over low heat. In a mixing bowl, break up 9 of the eggs with a fork, and season them with 1 teaspoon salt and some pepper. Add to the pan and stir gently with the back of a wooden fork, or with a wooden spoon, for 4 to 5 minutes, until they have softly set. Scrape the bottom and sides of the skillet continuously as you cook the eggs, to keep them as smooth as possible. Remove from the heat while still creamy and beat in the remaining egg to stop the cooking. Stir in the tomato and garlic flavoring; taste for seasoning.

Blot away any water exuded from the insides of the tomatoes. Spoon the scrambled eggs into the tomatoes; they should be filled to the top. Garnish each tomato with a slice of hard-boiled egg, a few of the capers, 2 strips of anchovy fillet, and the remaining basil leaves. The filled tomatoes are now ready to serve, or they can wait for 6 to 8 hours, covered with plastic wrap, in the refrigerator. One-half hour before serving, remove to room temperature. Serve from a platter nicely garnished with the lettuce leaves and cherry tomatoes.

Couronne de soles aux épinards, sauce beurre blanc

TURBAN OF SOLE WITH SPINACH
AND WHITE BUTTER SAUCE

For 8:

¾ pound (340 g) fresh spinach, trimmed of stems and washed
1 pound (450 g) boneless fish fillets—red snapper, sea bass, whitefish, etc
3 eggs
5 ounces (140 g) cream cheese, preferably without gum additives, at room temperature
⅓ cup (¾ dL) heavy cream

2 tablespoons chopped fresh parsley, or parsley and chervil
1 teaspoon *herbes de Provence* (see page 220)
1½ teaspoons salt
Freshly ground pepper
Freshly grated nutmeg
½ pound (225 g) sole fillets
Le beurre blanc de Simca (see below)

Recommended equipment: A food processor equipped with the metal blade (or a food mill); a 1½-quart (1½ L) ring mold

Butter the mold well. Cook the spinach in boiling salted water for 3 to 4 minutes, until just tender. Drain and refresh under cold running water, then drain again thoroughly and squeeze very dry either with your hands or in the corner of a strong kitchen towel.

To prepare in a food processor, cut the snapper or bass into 4 or 5 pieces, saving any trimmings for the sauce, then purée in the processor. If not fine enough put through the medium disk of a food mill, and turn into a bowl. In the processor, beat together the eggs, cream cheese, heavy cream, herbs, seasonings, and spinach. Then stir in the fish. (To prepare by hand, chop the fish fine and put through the medium disk of a food mill. Beat in the eggs. Blend the cream cheese with the heavy cream, then add to the fish, along with the herbs and seasonings. Chop the spinach finely with a knife and add it to the mixture.) Taste carefully for seasoning.

Trim the sole fillets into 8 long strips about ¾ inch wide and 7 inches long (2 cm x 18 cm). If they are more than ¼ inch (⅔ cm) thick, you may moisten them slightly and flatten with a cleaver or heavy knife. Season with salt and pepper and arrange evenly spaced in the mold, skin (shiny) side up, with their ends hanging over the sides of the mold. Pack the fish mousse firmly into the mold by spoonfuls, then fold the fillets over the mousse and give the mold several sharp taps on a flat surface to help settle the mixture. This may be covered with plastic wrap and set in the refrigerator for several hours or overnight. Remove it to room temperature 1 hour before you are ready to bake it.

Set the prepared mold in a pan of simmering water to come one-third of the way up its sides, and bake in a 400°F (205°C) oven for 25 to 30 minutes, until the mousse has firmed up and a knife inserted in the center comes out clean. Allow to cool for 5 or 10 minutes before unmolding onto a warm serving platter. If you wish to keep the dish warm for 30 to 40 minutes, allow it to remain in the hot water bath at room temperature. The dish can also be baked several hours in advance, partially rewarmed in the water bath at a simmer, and then heated in a 375°F (190°C) oven for 8 to 10 minutes.

Serve with the following sauce:

Le beurre blanc de Simca
WHITE WINE AND BUTTER SAUCE

For 1½ cups (3½ dL):

1 medium carrot, sliced
1 small onion, peeled and sliced
Bouquet garni—parsley, fresh or
    dried thyme, bay leaf
Any trimmings from the sole or
    other fish fillets
1 bottle dry white wine
1 tablespoon minced shallots

12 tablespoons (170 g) unsalted
    butter, cut into cubes and
    chilled
12 tablespoons (170 g) unsalted
    butter, at room temperature
A few drops of lemon juice
3 to 4 tablespoons heavy cream
1 teaspoon salt
Freshly ground pepper

In a medium-sized saucepan, simmer the carrots, onion, *bouquet garni,* and fish trimmings in the wine for about 30 minutes. Strain the liquid into a smaller saucepan. Add the minced shallots and continue reducing the liquid to about 4 tablespoons. Over low heat, whisk in the chilled butter all at once, then off heat beat in the remaining butter in small amounts, to make a smooth sauce. Add a few drops of lemon juice and stir in the cream. Season with the salt and pepper. The sauce may be served at once, or may wait for 20 to 30 minutes. When you are ready to serve, rewarm by whisking over hot water.

Tartes jumelles aux fruits tricolores
TWIN RED-WHITE-AND-BLUE RASPBERRY AND BLUEBERRY TARTS

For two 8- to 9-inch (20–23 cm) tarts, serving 8:

1 recipe *pâte sublime,* page 213
1 pint (240 g) fresh raspberries
1 pint (240 g) blueberries
⅓ cup (65 g) granulated sugar
⅓ cup (¾ dL) heavy cream

2 tablespoons powdered sugar, plus powdered sugar in a shaker
¼ cup (½ dL) Cointreau or other orange liqueur
½ cup (1 dL) red-currant jelly

Recommended equipment: 2 eight- to nine-inch (20–23 cm) false-bottomed tart tins

Make the pastry, then line the tart tins and set them in the freezer to chill, as directed in the recipe for *tarte aux pommes Mirliton* on page 117. When the pastry is firm, set the tart tins on a baking sheet and bake in a 450°F (230°C) oven for 4 to 5 minutes, to precook the pastry. Prick the pastry with a fork if it puffs up. Reduce the heat to 375°F (190°C). Bake one shell for another 8 to 10 minutes until the bottom feels firm and dry (the edges will have browned slightly). Remove to a cooling rack. Allow the other tart shell to bake fully for 10 to 15 minutes more, until it is a nice golden brown all over. Remove to a rack also. The tart shells, in their tins, may wait for several hours or overnight, uncovered and at room temperature, before the tarts are assembled.

Pick over the berries. It is best not to wash the raspberries, to avoid bruising them. Add the blueberries to the partially baked shell (still in its tin). Sprinkle on the granulated sugar and bake in a 400°F (205°C) oven for 40 to 45 minutes, until the fruit is tender and its juice has reduced and become slightly syrupy; stir once or twice delicately with a wooden fork to blend the berries and sugar. If the pastry browns too quickly, cover loosely with a piece of foil. Set on a rack to cool.

Whip the cream with the 2 tablespoons powdered sugar. When it is nearly stiff, add 2 tablespoons of the orange liqueur and continue beating until firm. Melt the red-currant jelly with the rest of the liqueur, stirring it over heat until it boils and is a smooth glaze. Allow to cool and thicken slightly.

Paint the bottom of the fully baked tart shell with a layer of glaze, using a pastry brush. Spoon in the whipped cream and spread it evenly to the sides. Arrange the whole raspberries in a neat and attractive single layer on top of the cream. Paint half of the raspberry tart with the remaining glaze; dust the other half heavily with powdered sugar (use a large chef's knife as a guide for the sugar). Dust half of the blueberry tart heavily with powdered sugar.

Remove the tarts from the tins onto a cutting surface. Slice each one into 8 serving pieces, starting with a cut across the line of sugar. Now, working on two serving platters, reassemble two separate tarts, alternating slices of white with red and then blue.

The tarts will be at their best if served within an hour or two.

Un dîner prié

A DINNER FOR SPECIAL GUESTS, FOR 8

Timbales de foies de volaille
UNMOLDED CHICKEN-LIVER TIMBALES

Bordeaux—Haut Brion/Robert Mondavi
Cabernet Sauvignon

Les chaudrées pitchounes
INDIVIDUAL MARMITES OF SEAFOOD
WITH CREAMY LEEKS

Salade verte et un plateau de fromages
GREEN SALAD AND CHEESE

Le Moka
BITTERSWEET FROZEN MOCHA SOUFFLÉ

vin blanc de Nice—Bellet/Freemark Abbey
Pinot Chardonnay

Un dîner prié

This could be a menu for a group of hand-picked friends, to whom a favor or a dinner is owed. The dishes are all elegant and require a certain care—they are *cousu main*. To begin the dinner are very smooth mousselines, whose individual servings make a gracious presentation. Instructions are also given for baking the dish in a ring mold, which is perhaps an easier method but also a little less dressy. It is served with a red wine sauce, making a nice balance with the creamy richness of the fish to follow.

The idea for this main-course dish originated in a meal I shared with a distinguished club of gastronomes dedicated to fish—L'Association des Gastronomes Amateurs de Poisson! We used to lunch at Prunier's, that famous fish restaurant in Paris, which on this occasion served a wonderful specialty called *marmite dieppoise*. This was an elegant chowder filled with beautiful seafood—plenty of crab, *langoustine,* and what we call *poissons nobles,* the finest kinds of fish, such as turbot and sole. The memory of this and, several years later, of a special leek sauce with truffles, cooked by one of the world's great chefs, Frédy Girardet, inspired the dish that I call *les chaudrées pitchounes.*

In the Provençal dialect, *pitchoune* means "little thing" (and it is the name that Paul and Julia Child chose for their charming vacation house, just near ours). But *pitchoune* can also describe these miniature arrangements of seafood in individual ovenproof bowls, which I like to serve not only as a delicate course for a dinner party, but also for a luncheon. It is a complete main-course dish, with a choice of fresh fish fillets, and any shellfish or mollusks in season, all arranged on a creamy bed of truffled leeks and then gently poached. Of course, the truffles are optional, but they are wonderful combined with the leeks.

You may also serve this dish from one large terrine, but I think that it is rather more fun to allow each guest his own bowl.

Le Moka is an impressive dessert to present after salad and cheese. The deep flavors of coffee and bitter cocoa are softened by a parfait base of thickened egg yolks and cream, with beaten egg whites added for lightness. And although the dessert can be made in advance, it will really be at its best if eaten within 4 or 5 hours of setting it in the freezer, while the center is still slightly soft.

Timbales de foies de volaille

UNMOLDED CHICKEN-LIVER TIMBALES

For 8:

2 medium-sized shallots, peeled	3 tablespoons Cognac
1 clove garlic, peeled	8 eggs
4 or 5 sprigs parsley, washed and dried	2 tablespoons potato starch or arrowroot
3 tablespoons (45 g) butter	2 cups (½ L) heavy cream
2 teaspoons *herbes de Provence* (see page 220)	2 teaspoons salt
	Freshly ground pepper
1 pound (450 g) chicken livers	*Sauce Morgon* (see below)

Recommended equipment: Eight 1-cup (¼ L) metal baba molds (or porcelain ramequins)

Place a circle of buttered waxed paper on the bottom of each baba cup, then heavily butter the sides. Make a *persillade* by chopping the shallots, garlic, and parsley either in a food processor or with a knife. Melt the butter in a large skillet, then add the *persillade* and the *herbes de Provence* and sauté gently over medium-low heat for 2 or 3 minutes, stirring from time to time.

Pick over the chicken livers, removing any stringy bits. Add the livers to the skillet and stir them over medium-low heat for 3 to 4 minutes, until they are just lightly colored; they will finish cooking in the oven. Pour on the Cognac and ignite, to burn off the alcohol. Remove and purée in a food processor or with a food mill. Beat the eggs with the potato starch and cream, just to blend them, and stir in the chicken liver mixture, together with the salt and pepper. Turn into the prepared molds, which may wait for 1 hour at room temperature before baking. If you wish, you may refrigerate them several hours covered with plastic wrap; an hour before baking, remove to room temperature.

To finish the timbales, set them in simmering water that comes one-third of the way up their sides, then bake in a 375°F (190°C) oven for 15 to 20 minutes, until they have puffed slightly and are fairly firm to the touch. They may, however, remain a little soft in the center. Allow to cool for a minute or two before unmolding one by one onto a hot serving platter or directly onto hot plates. Remove the waxed paper and then top with some of the hot *sauce Morgon* (see below). Pass any remaining sauce in a sauceboat.

Variation: Savarin de foies de volaille (Chicken livers in a ring mold). To make in a 6-cup (1½ L) ring mold, heavily butter the mold and pour in the prepared mixture. Place in simmering water that comes one-third of the way up its sides, and then bake in a 375°F (190°C) oven for 25 to 30 minutes, until a knife inserted in the liver comes out clean. Allow to cool for 10 to 15 minutes before unmolding.

Sauce Morgon
RED WINE SAUCE WITH
SHALLOTS AND MADEIRA

For about 2 cups (½ L):

½ bottle fruity red wine—a
  Beaujolais or Zinfandel
3 medium-sized shallots, peeled
  and minced
2 teaspoons *herbes de Provence*
  (see page 220)
2 cups (½ L) chicken stock

2 teaspoons potato starch or
  arrowroot
⅓ cup (¾ dL) dry Madeira
Salt and freshly ground pepper
  to taste
4 tablespoons (60 g) cool butter

74

Place the wine, shallots, and *herbes de Provence* in a medium-sized saucepan and boil until the wine has reduced by half. Add the chicken stock and continue reducing until you have about 1½ cups (3½ dL). Dissolve the starch with a few drops of the Madeira, then stir in the rest of the wine and whisk it into the simmering liquid. Continue simmering until thickened to a nice consistency, for another 4 to 5 minutes. Off heat, whisk in the butter by tablespoons and season carefully.

To prepare the sauce in advance, omit the butter enrichment and set the sauce aside at room temperature, or in the refrigerator for a longer wait. When ready to serve, bring the sauce to a simmer, then proceed to add the butter enrichment and seasoning, as above.

Les chaudrées pitchounes

INDIVIDUAL MARMITES OF SEAFOOD
WITH CREAMY LEEKS

For 8:

2 pounds (900 g) leeks
12 tablespoons (170 g) butter
2½ teaspoons salt
Freshly ground pepper
2 cups (½ L) heavy cream
1 ounce (30 g) black truffle, cut into fine julienne
1 pound (450 g) fillet of sole
2 pounds (900 g) other boneless fish fillets—red snapper, salmon, trout, lake whitefish, sea bass, etc.
8 of any of the following— prawns, crayfish, *langoustine,* or scallops (optional)
8 fresh mussels or clams, in their shells, well scrubbed (optional)
¾ bottle light white wine—a Sancerre or California Fumé Blanc

Recommended equipment: 8 ovenproof bowls or soup plates, of at least 1½-cup (3½ dL) capacity

75

Lightly butter the bowls. Trim the leeks of their tough or dirty greens and the roots, slit them lengthwise, and wash thoroughly under cold running water. Chop coarsely, then melt the butter in a heavy-bottomed saucepan or skillet, add the leeks, and cook gently in the butter, covered, for 8 to 10 minutes, stirring occasionally. Uncover and continue cooking over medium-low heat until nearly tender, 3 to 4 minutes more. Season with a teaspoon of the salt and a bit of pepper. Add half the cream, along with the truffle and its juice, if canned. Allow the cream to simmer for 4 to 5 minutes, until it has reduced and thickened slightly. Correct the seasoning; divide the leek mixture evenly among the 8 bowls.

Trim the sole fillets into 8 long strips about 1½ inches (4 cm) wide; moisten with wine and flatten them slightly with a cleaver or large knife. Season, roll up loosely, and place one in the center of each bowl. Trim the remaining fish fillets into 16 neat pieces of about 2 ounces (60 g) each, season, and also divide evenly among the bowls. If you are not using any of the optional shellfish or mollusks, the *chaudrées* are ready.

If you are using prawns or shrimp, remove the shells and reserve. If you are using live crayfish or *langoustine,* drop them for 1 minute into boiling water, then run them under cold water before removing their tail meat; again reserve the shells. Whatever optional garnish you have chosen, season it lightly and place it over the sole *paupiette.* Complete the *chaudrée* by standing either a whole mussel or clam in each bowl. Once assembled, the *chaudrées* may wait for several hours in the refrigerator. About 30 minutes before baking them, remove to room temperature.

In a saucepan, boil the wine, with any of the shells, until it has reduced by one-third. Add the remaining cream and simmer the liquid for another minute or two. Strain and season carefully; you should have about 2 cups (½ L). Divide the broth evenly among the 8 bowls, then cover each bowl tightly with foil and place on baking sheets. Bake in a 375°F (190°C) oven for 18 to 20 minutes, until the fish is just done but not dry and the mussels or clams, if you have used them, are beginning to open. Serve at once.

Le Moka

BITTERSWEET FROZEN MOCHA SOUFFLÉ

For 8 to 10:

3 tablespoons instant coffee
  granules
5 tablespoons dark rum
5 tablespoons water
¾ cup (85 g) unsweetened
  cocoa

6 eggs, separated
1 cup (190 g) granulated sugar
¼ teaspoon salt
2 cups (½ L) heavy cream
1 teaspoon vanilla extract

Recommended equipment: A 1½-quart (1½ L) porcelain soufflé dish, fitted with an aluminum foil or waxed paper collar extending 2 to 3 inches (5 to 8 cm) above dish; an electric mixer

In a small bowl, dissolve the coffee in the rum and water, then mix in the cocoa and whisk until smooth; the mixture will be rather thick. Set aside.

Beat the egg yolks in a medium-sized metal mixing bowl until they have thickened slightly and are pale in color. Place ⅔ cup (125 g) of the sugar in a small saucepan with 3 tablespoons of water and cook it over moderate heat for 2 to 3 minutes, until it boils to the thread stage; the syrup should just run in a sticky stream from the tip of a metal spoon. Beating the egg yolks at high speed with the electric mixer, pour on the boiling syrup in a steady stream, slowly at first and then more rapidly as the yolks warm through. Continue beating until thickened and cold; you may do this more quickly by setting the bowl in ice water. Add the coffee-cocoa mixture, beating for 30 seconds or so until well blended. Set aside.

Beat the egg whites with the salt until they form soft peaks. Then add the remaining ⅓ cup (65 g) sugar and continue beating until firm peaks are formed. Whip the cream until it is stiff. Fold the mocha-egg yolk mixture into the meringue, then fold in the whipped cream. Pour into the prepared mold and set in the freezer for 4 to 5 hours, if you wish to serve it with a slightly creamy center. The dessert can be prepared and frozen a day or two ahead, but it will, of course, be firm all the way through and more like an ice cream.

When you are ready to serve the dessert, remove the collar and decorate attractively in any way you wish: with chocolate curls or with whipped cream piped through a star pastry tip; or you can sprinkle the surface heavily with powdered sugar and press a cooling rack into the sugar in different ways to make a pretty pattern. Serve by cutting the upper portion into wedges and spooning out the rest.

Menus with Poultry

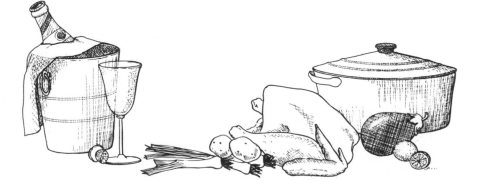

MAIN DISHES:

Poulet en persillade

Suprêmes de dinde à la Champvallon

Canards au citron et au whiskey

Poulet en roulade

Lapin et deux volailles en gelée

Un déjeuner versatile

A VERSATILE LUNCH FOR 6

Soufflé (ou timbale) forestière
ARTICHOKE AND MUSHROOM SOUFFLÉ
(OR TIMBALE)

Poulet en persillade
CHICKEN BAKED WITH MUSTARD, PARSLEY,
AND GARLIC, IN A CREAM SAUCE

Paillasson de pommes de terre
CRISP GRATED POTATO GALETTE

Clafoutis aux prunes ou aux cerises de Bramafam
FRESH PLUMS OR CHERRIES BAKED IN
CREAM-CHEESE CUSTARD

Châteauneuf-du-Pape / Mt. Veeder Malbec

Un déjeuner versatile

A VERSATILE LUNCH FOR 6

This is a good menu for cooks with their own ideas, one that can be made for a simple occasion or easily dressed up with a clever touch or two. The *soufflé forestière,* for instance, is a very elegant first course for an important lunch, but for an everyday meal it can be made as a timbale, baked well ahead of time and then reheated. To accompany the chicken *en persillade,* the crisp and delicious potato *paillasson* is really all that is needed. Should you wish a green vegetable as well, I recommend the *courgettes à la Campanette* on page 13, whose cooking broth can be boiled down and added to the cream sauce for the chicken, to give it a touch of the vegetable's lovely flavor. The *clafoutis* is a rather homey dessert, and if you prefer a fancier finish to the meal you could serve it with an elegant sauce of sieved raspberries.

For making the soufflé, a *bouillie* (white sauce without butter) is used, and I do believe that this gives a very light result. Also, since the flavors of artichoke and mushroom in the soufflé are delicate, no cheese is added. The cooking of the mushrooms *à blanc*—with evaporated milk, keeping the mushrooms creamy and white—is still my preferred method. The artichokes are quite easily done; here, only the bottoms are used. For the timbale variation—where the *bouillie* is omitted altogether—only the egg yolks and beaten whites are combined with the vegetable purées, and the flavors are rather more rich. The texture, too, is different from that of the soufflé, a little less creamy but still delicate.

In any menu, I think it is always useful to have one quick but still tasty dish, and the *poulet en persillade* is just that, involving no browning or other preliminary steps. The pieces of chicken are simply coated with a nicely flavored herb mustard (I like tarragon) and then baked with plenty of parsley, some garlic, a little broth, and good wine vinegar, which all become the base for a savory, light cream sauce thickened by a slight reduction. It is a marvelous dish to have in your repertoire, as it can be ready for the table nearly 1 hour after it is begun, with the sauce practically making itself. Some people might prefer a more delicate flavor in the *persillade,* in which case it can be sautéed for 1 or 2 minutes in a little oil before it is sprinkled on the chicken.

The name of the potato dish in this menu comes from its resemblance to a straw door mat—*paillasson*—and it is one of my favorite ways to do crisp potatoes for a party. It is so very easy to grate the potatoes in a food processor and then cook the *paillasson* in advance, to be crisped and reheated at the last minute. As for the *clafoutis,* it is a nice, simple dessert for the summer months, when fresh fruit is plentiful and sweet. Apart from plums or cherries, you could use peaches, apricots, even figs. But during the other seasons any kind of tasty stewed or baked fruit mixture would be good with the custard: apples or pears, or even fresh sliced kiwi.

Soufflé forestière

ARTICHOKE AND MUSHROOM SOUFFLÉ

For 6:

6 large fresh artichokes, trimmed of the stems and tips of their leaves
1 recipe creamy minced mushrooms, page 219
4 tablespoons (60 g) butter
3 tablespoons finely minced shallots
Salt

Freshly ground pepper
Freshly grated nutmeg
¼ cup (35 g) flour
1 cup (¼ L) milk
3 eggs, separated, plus 2 extra whites
Pinch of cream of tartar (optional)

83

Recommended equipment: A 6-cup (1½ L) porcelain soufflé dish

Plunge the artichokes into a large quantity of boiling salted water and cook them until a knife inserted in the bottom of an artichoke pierces it easily. Drain the artichokes; refresh them in cold water, then drain again, thoroughly. Remove all of the leaves and the chokes, and purée the bottoms in a food processor or put them through the fine disk of a food mill; you should have about ¾ cup. Set aside. Prepare the mushrooms as directed.

Melt the butter in a medium-sized skillet and add the shallots, stirring them over low heat until they begin to be tender, about 2 to 3 minutes. Add the mushroom and artichoke purées and stir over heat for another 2 or 3 minutes until their flavors are well blended. Off heat, season the mixture with ¾ teaspoon salt, and pepper and nutmeg to taste.

Place the flour in a medium-sized saucepan and gradually whisk in the milk, adding it by tablespoonfuls at first to make a smooth paste, then more rapidly to thin it out. Add 1 teaspoon salt and a dash of pepper and nutmeg, and whisk constantly over medium-high heat until the liquid thickens to a smooth sauce. Stir over heat a minute or two longer to cook the flour slightly, then off heat stir in the egg yolks, one at a time Stir in the mushroom and artichoke purées; correct the seasoning. The prepared soufflé base may now wait for 1 or 2 hours at room temperature, with a piece of plastic wrap pressed directly onto its surface to prevent a skin from forming.

When you are ready to cook the soufflé, butter the baking dish well. Beat the egg whites with a pinch of salt (and a pinch of cream of tartar if you are not beating in a copper bowl) until they form stiff but not dry peaks. Stir the soufflé base over medium heat until it is warmed through, then fold it delicately into the whites. Pour into the prepared soufflé dish and bake in a 400°F (205°C) oven for 20 to 25 minutes. The soufflé should puff an inch or two (2½–5 cm) above the rim of the dish and be a nice golden brown. The center is delicious if it remains slightly soft, so don't allow the soufflé to overcook. Serve at once.

Variation: Timbale d'Artichauts et de Champignons (Artichoke and mushroom timbale).

The blended artichoke and
  mushroom purées (see above)
4 eggs, separated, plus 1 extra
  egg white

Finely chopped fresh parsley
Pinch of salt
Pinch of cream of tartar
  (optional)

Recommended equipment: A 6-cup (1½ L) metal charlotte mold (or similar mold)

Line the bottom of the mold with waxed paper if it is to be unmolded, and butter the entire mold well. Blend the egg yolks with the warm vegetable purées (if you have done them in advance, warm them over gentle heat before adding the yolks); correct the seasoning. Beat the egg whites with a pinch of salt (and a pinch of cream of tartar if you are not beating in a copper bowl), then delicately fold in the vegetable purée. Pour the mixture into the prepared mold and bake it in a 375°F (190°C) oven for 20 to 25 minutes. The timbale will puff slightly, to just appear over the top of the mold. Either unmold the dish or spoon it directly from the mold.

Poulet en persillade

CHICKEN BAKED WITH MUSTARD, PARSLEY,
AND GARLIC, IN A CREAM SAUCE

For 6:

2 fine, fresh chickens each 3½ to 4 pounds (1500–1800 g), cut into serving pieces

2 to 3 tablespoons tarragon mustard or Dijon mustard flavored with 1 teaspoon chopped fresh tarragon or ½ teaspoon dried

6 cloves garlic, peeled

8 to 10 large sprigs of parsley

1 cup (¼ L) concentrated chicken broth (made from a bouillon cube, if you wish)

3 tablespoons red wine vinegar

⅔ c (1½ dL) heavy cream

Salt and freshly ground pepper, as needed

1 teaspoon chopped fresh tarragon or parsley (optional)

Recommended equipment: An ovenproof dish (such as enameled cast-iron), large enough to hold the pieces of chicken in one layer

Pat the pieces of chicken dry and coat them generously with the mustard. Finely chop the garlic and parsley together in a food processor or with a knife. Pour the chicken broth and the vinegar into the bottom of the baking dish; sprinkle in half of the *persillade*—the chopped garlic and parsley. Arrange the chicken in the dish and sprinkle with the remaining *persillade*. Cover with a piece of buttered foil. The dish can now wait for an hour or so at room temperature before baking.

Bring the liquid in the dish to a simmer on top of the stove, then bake the chicken in a 375°F (190°C) oven for 35 to 40 minutes. Turn the pieces once or twice as they cook; you may remove the pieces of white meat from the oven 5 minutes sooner than the dark, as they tend to cook faster. The chicken is done when it is fairly firm to the finger, still moist, and only faintly pink at the bone; it should not over-cook or it will be dry.

Transfer to a serving platter and keep warm in the turned-off oven (about 200°F, or 95°C). Pour the heavy cream into the baking dish, stir it well to deglaze the baking juices, and reduce over medium-high heat. If you have made the *courgettes à la Campanette* on page 13, reduce the reserved cooking liquid to about ½ cup (1 dL) and add it to the simmering sauce for the chicken. After 8 to 10 minutes you should have a sauce of a nice consistency; taste it for seasoning. Pour a bit of the sauce over the pieces of chicken and sprinkle with the chopped fresh tarragon or parsley. Pass the remaining sauce in a sauce-boat.

To prepare the dish an hour or two in advance, cook the chicken for 30 minutes, then remove it to an ovenproof platter and cover it with foil (remove the breast meat 5 minutes before the dark meat). Finish the sauce as directed and pour it into a saucepan. Twenty minutes before serving, place the chicken in a 350°F (180°C) oven to finish its cooking and warm it through. Reheat the sauce and serve with the chicken as directed above.

Paillasson de pommes de terre
CRISP GRATED POTATO GALETTE

For 6:

1¼ pounds (565 g) boiling
  potatoes
3 tablespoons peanut oil
6 tablespoons (85 g) butter

1 teaspoon salt
Freshly ground pepper
1 teaspoon chopped fresh parsley

Recommended equipment: A food processor equipped with the coarse grating blade (or a hand grater); a 12-inch (30 cm) nonstick skillet

Peel the potatoes and grate them coarsely, either in the food processor or with a hand grater. Wash them in two or three changes of cold water—by rinsing away the potato starch, the center of the *paillasson* will be light and creamy rather than gluey—then drain and pat thoroughly dry in a towel.

In the skillet, heat the oil and 3 tablespoons (45 g) butter, then add the potatoes; they should sizzle as they touch the hot fat. Using a wooden spoon or metal spatula, press the potatoes into a neat and even layer to completely fill the bottom of the skillet and form the *paillasson*. Brown over medium-low heat for 15 to 20 minutes, then season with ½ teaspoon salt and a bit of pepper. Slip onto a large plate, add the remaining butter to the pan, and invert the *paillasson* back into the skillet to finishing browning on the other side, for 10 to 15 minutes more. Season with the remaining ½ teaspoon salt and more pepper.

Slip the crisp potatoes onto a cutting board and slice into wedges. With the help of two large spatulas or the false bottom from a tart tin, transfer to a warm serving platter, sprinkle with the parsley, and serve.

To do the *paillasson* ahead of time, finish its cooking and slip it onto a large plate or platter to wait. Just before serving, melt 3 tablespoons (45 g) of fresh butter in the skillet and crisp the potatoes on both sides over medium-high heat.

Clafoutis aux prunes ou aux cerises de Bramafam

FRESH PLUMS OR CHERRIES BAKED IN
CREAM-CHEESE CUSTARD

For 6:

1 pound (450 g) fresh ripe
  plums or cherries
5 tablespoons water

⅔ cup (125 g) granulated sugar
5 tablespoons (70 g) unsalted
  butter, at room temperature

6 ounces (170 g) cream cheese,
    preferably without gum
    additives—also at room
    temperature
⅓ cup (¾ dL) heavy cream
2 eggs

3 tablespoons flour
2 tablespoons potato starch
2 tablespoons imported kirsch
Grated zest of 1 lime or lemon
Powdered sugar, in a shaker

Recommended equipment: A 12-inch (30 cm) oval baking dish

Wash the plums, halve them, and remove their pits. If you are using cherries, wash and pit them and slice them in half. Place in a medium-sized saucepan with the water and 2 tablespoons of the sugar and cook over medium-low heat, partially covered, for 20 minutes, stirring occasionally. Uncover the pan and cook for another 10 minutes or so. The fruit should reduce to a tender compote. Set aside.

While the fruit is cooking, prepare the custard. In a food processor or with an electric beater, blend the butter with the cream cheese and the heavy cream. Beat in the eggs, then the remaining sugar and the flour, potato starch, kirsch, and grated rind.

Butter the baking dish. Spread half of the custard mixture in the bottom of the dish, then spoon in the stewed fruit in an even layer. Pour on the remaining custard, and give it a good sprinkle of powdered sugar (about 1 to 2 tablespoons). Bake in a 400°F (205°C) oven for 30 to 35 minutes. The custard should just set and its surface turn lightly golden. Allow to cool for at least 30 minutes before serving. Serve tepid or cold, dusted lightly with more of the powdered sugar, and spooned onto plates.

Un menu confortable

A COZY MENU FOR 8

Rarebit à la française
FRENCH RAREBIT

Suprêmes de dinde à la Champvallon
SLICED TURKEY BREAST BAKED UNDER
POTATOES AND CREAM

Salade de coeurs de romaine
HEARTS OF ROMAINE IN VINAIGRETTE

Soufflé Harriet, au chocolat
AN EASY CHOCOLATE SOUFFLÉ

une folie de Champagne/Domaine Chandon Brut
or
vin blanc de la Loire—Condrieu/Callaway Vineyards
Sauvignon Blanc Fumé

Un menu confortable

When I was a young woman in Paris—long before I had any notion of a career in cooking—nights about the capital city were gay and exciting, and I remember one of my favorite restaurants for a snack after shopping, or a good supper after the theatre, was a very lively place on the rue Royale, the Café Weber. It was a gathering spot for *le tout Paris,* quite elegant, and yet one could relax there and have a splendid time with friends. One of the things we often ate was piping hot Welsh rarebit, that classic fondue of Cheddar cheese on toast. I myself loved this cozy dish with champagne, close to midnight when the fun was at its best. Now, of course, my dear Paris has changed so much, and there are no more fabulous nights at the Weber, which has gone. But the memory remains and has inspired me, many years later, to create my own *rarebit à la française.*

This thick cheese sauce made with white wine resembles the fondue of Switzerland, while the flavoring of Worcestershire sauce is derived from the original dish. But the "rarebit" becomes very French with the addition of a good Comté cheese (although a Swiss type can be used), and its flavoring of Dijon mustard and a bit of Cognac. It is easy to do an hour or so ahead of time, and although the fondue will become quite thick and heavy as it cools, when rewarmed it becomes light again. This *rarebit français* is good, too, with drinks, if the toast is trimmed into bite-sized triangles after it has browned with the cheese.

The turkey dish *à la Champvallon* comes from a classic preparation with veal, but since I often like to search beyond the classic, I recreated the recipe with turkey breast, which is also a white meat and yet so much more available than veal in the United States. In its gratin with cream and potatoes, which are precooked so as not to overcook the meat, the turkey makes a nourishing and complete course in itself, and if properly done should be very juicy. Although I find that a green salad complements this main course quite nicely, you could add a green vegetable if you wish—for example, the green bean purée on page 6.

For so many of my cooking ideas I am indebted to my students, and to almost no one more than my wonderful friend Harriet Healy. Harriet was the very first student to come to Julia Child and me when our Paris school was born in 1953. Since then, she has become a great cook who has created many clever ideas for French cooking done with American ingredients, and this easy chocolate soufflé is of her invention. It really could not be simpler, as it is no more than a chocolate *béchamel* with beaten egg whites, which can be cooked in any kind of shallow ovenproof dish of about 2½ quarts (2½ L). This soufflé, I have found, always works. It puffs prettily, and because it is baked over a much larger surface than a regular soufflé, you haven't the worry of its spilling over or of making a collar. Also, it seems to cook more evenly and does not sink so fast. In fact, it hardly sinks at all by the time it is served.

For this menu I have specified *une folie de champagne*—the extravagant pouring of lovely sparkling wine to accompany the rarebit, but this is only an idea, and you could certainly serve the still white wine throughout the meal.

Rarebit à la française

FRENCH RAREBIT

For 8:

8 slices *pain de mie au lait,* page 215, or any other good white bread, about ⅜ inch (1 cm) thick
4 tablespoons (60 g) butter, at room temperature
¾ pound (340 g) French Comté or Beaufort cheese, or a good Swiss cheese
2 tablespoons flour
1⅓ cups (3¼ dL) dry white wine

1 small clove of garlic, peeled and minced
1 tablespoon Dijon mustard
¼ teaspoon salt
Freshly ground pepper
Freshly grated nutmeg
Pinch of cayenne or a few drops of Tabasco
2 teaspoons Worcestershire sauce
2 tablespoons Cognac

Recommended equipment: 2 large oval gratin dishes (or any other flat ovenproof dishes) large enough to hold the slices of bread in 1 layer

Toast the slices of bread on both sides under a medium-hot broiler, then spread them with the butter. Set the canapés in the gratin dishes and return them to the turned-off oven to continue drying while you work on the fondue.

Grate the cheese in a food processor or by hand. Toss it in a bowl with the flour. Bring the wine and garlic to a simmer in a medium-sized heavy-bottomed saucepan and cook for a minute or two over medium heat to evaporate some of the alcohol. Using a wooden spoon, stir in the cheese until smooth, a few tablespoons at a time. Then stir in all the remaining ingredients. Continue stirring for 1 or 2 minutes more, to blend all of the flavors, then remove the pan from the heat. Correct the seasoning.

If ready to serve, pour the fondue over the buttered canapés. Or it can wait for an hour or so at room temperature and then be reheated and stirred until creamy and smooth again. Run the completed dish under a hot broiler until it is bubbling and lightly browned.

Suprêmes de dinde à la Champvallon

SLICED TURKEY BREAST BAKED UNDER
POTATOES AND CREAM

For 8:

1 whole turkey breast, 5 to 6 pounds (2¼–2¾ kg) to make about 3 pounds (1350 g) boned and skinned
4 tablespoons (60 g) butter
¼ cup (½ dL) cooking oil
½ cup (1 dL) turkey or chicken broth (or broth made from a bouillon cube)
Salt and freshly ground pepper
2 pounds (900 g) onions, peeled and sliced

3 cups (¾ L) milk
2 pounds (900 g) boiling potatoes, peeled and cut into ⅛-inch (⅓ cm) slices
Freshly grated nutmeg
1 clove garlic, peeled
1 teaspoon *herbes de Provence* (see page 220)
½ cup (1 dL) heavy cream
A handful of parsley, chopped

Recommended equipment: A large nonstick skillet; a large (14-inch [35 cm]) oval gratin dish

Cut the turkey into 16 to 18 nice slices about ⅜ inch (1 cm) thick, and pat them dry with paper towels. Heat half each of the butter and oil in the skillet and lightly sear the slices of turkey over moderate

95

heat, four or five at a time, for 30 to 40 seconds on each side; remove to a large platter or tray. When all of the slices are done, pour out the fat from the pan, deglaze with 2 to 3 tablespoons of the broth and pour over the meat. Season with salt and pepper.

Heat the remaining butter and oil in the skillet. Add the onions and stir them for a minute or two over medium heat to coat them with the fat. Cover, reduce the heat, and cook for 20 to 30 minutes, stirring from time to time, until very tender and sweet. Uncover during the last 5 minutes of cooking to evaporate any excess moisture, and season the onions lightly.

While the onions cook bring the milk and the potatoes to a boil with 2 teaspoons salt and a bit of nutmeg. Cook at a gentle simmer, stirring frequently, for 12 to 15 minutes or until the potatoes are just tender.

Rub the gratin dish with the garlic. Put in a layer of half the onions, then make a layer of the turkey, overlapping each slice. Add the remaining onions, sprinkle on the herbs, and pour in the remaining chicken broth, along with any juices accumulated around the meat. Using a slotted spoon or skimmer, lift the potatoes out of the milk and spread them evenly over the turkey. Finally, pour the milk (which should have thickened and reduced to about 1 cup, or ¼ L) over all. The assembled dish may now wait for an hour or so at room temperature before finishing.

Dribble in the heavy cream and bake in a 400°F (205°C) oven for 15 to 18 minutes, to finish cooking the potatoes and warm the meat through. Run the dish under a hot broiler to brown it lightly. Sprinkle with the parsley and serve at once.

Soufflé Harriet, au chocolat

AN EASY CHOCOLATE SOUFFLÉ

For 8:

2 tablespoons (30 g) unsalted
   butter
3 tablespoons all-purpose flour
1½ cups (3½ dL) milk
7 ounces (200 g) semisweet
   chocolate, broken into bits
1 tablespoon instant coffee
   granules

¼ cup (½ dL) water
6 eggs, separated, plus 2 extra
   whites
Pinch of salt
¾ cup (145 g) granulated sugar
Powdered sugar, in a shaker

Recommended equipment: A 10- to 11-cup (2½ L) shallow oval
baking dish—Pyrex or enameled cast-iron

Butter the baking dish well. In a medium-sized saucepan melt the
butter, then whisk in the flour and stir over medium heat for a minute
or two to cook the flour. Off heat whisk in the cold milk, all at once.
Return the pan to the heat and bring the sauce to a simmer, whisking
gently until it thickens and is smooth.

Place the chocolate, coffee granules, and water in another larger,
heavy-bottomed saucepan; melt the chocolate over medium-low heat,
stirring occasionally until it is smooth. Off heat stir in the egg yolks,
then return the pan to the heat for a minute or two, stirring constantly, until the egg yolks are warmed and have thickened the
chocolate. Stir the *béchamel* into the melted chocolate, whisking until
the mixtures are well blended. This may now wait for an hour or two
at room temperature.

When ready to bake, stir the sauce over heat to rewarm it, if necessary. Beat the egg whites with a pinch of salt until they form soft
peaks. Gradually sprinkle on the granulated sugar as you continue

beating to firm peaks. Fold the warm sauce delicately into the egg whites, then pour the soufflé mixture into the baking dish. Bake in a 400°F (205°C) oven for 23 to 25 minutes for a soufflé with a slightly soft center, and 30 minutes for one that is rather more firm; the soufflé should rise an inch or two (2½–5 cm) above the rim of the dish. Sprinkle with powdered sugar and serve at once, spooning it onto warm plates.

Un menu pour épater les amis

A MENU TO DAZZLE YOUR FRIENDS, FOR 6

✶

Avocats en aspic
AVOCADOS IN ASPIC FLAVORED
WITH TARRAGON AND PORT

vin blanc de La Loire—
Pouilly Fumé/Rutherford Hill Chenin Blanc

Canards au citron et au whiskey
DUCKS WITH LEMON AND WHISKEY SAUCE

Les zéphyrs de pommes de terre
INDIVIDUAL POTATO MOUSSELINES

Le Savoureux
CHOCOLATE HAZELNUT GÉNOISE WITH
CINNAMON AND KIRSCH

Bordeaux rouge—Médoc/Beaulieu Private Reserve
Cabernet Sauvignon

Un menu pour épater les amis

I have planned this menu to entertain food-loving friends who deserve rich and elaborate dishes, and for whom you love to cook. At first glance the duck recipe might appear formidable, and my immediate advice is first to thoroughly familiarize yourself with the procedure for preparing this tasty dish. It contains no very difficult steps, and is frankly an excellent exercise in many techniques of French cooking: the preparation of a brown stock; the braising of the dark meat, which gives a very tender result; then the careful refinements to the sauce. The duck breasts are roasted separately at the last minute to keep them pink, and the fatty skin is discarded (although if you wished it could be sautéed until crisp, sliced and served with the dish); the breast meat is then sliced and served with the legs and thighs. This is a satisfactory treatment for duck, since *all* of the meat will be tender and juicy, and not at all fatty. So while in a sense the *canards* are an ambitious dish, something for the more experienced cook, if you proceed carefully nothing can fail. The flavoring for the ducks is a departure from the classic orange, which can be so tiresome. With the lemon, the brown sauce is rather more tart than sweet, and the whiskey gives a heady perfume.

To balance the last-minute work of the ducks, the first course and the dessert are cold dishes, and I would recommend that you prepare both of them the day before. With the avocados, again it is a question of working carefully with certain techniques, most especially the clarifying of stock for aspic. If you undertake this procedure well in advance, and patiently, you will be rewarded with a splendid result— a sparkling clear jelly, which is the basis for so many beautiful presentations of cold food. I must say that I am very fond of avocados, and they are so wonderful to buy in the United States compared to France, where the prices are almost like those for truffles! So you should take advantage of them.

The vegetable accompaniment in this menu—individual mousselines of potato—is very classic, and well worth doing. This dish contains, among other things, a profligate amount of butter! But when one tastes the results one must relent, for the flavors of potato and butter are known to be one of the great culinary combinations. If you would like to serve a green vegetable, I suggest the Brussels sprouts *à la Crécy* on page 28, but a simple green salad, after the duck but on the same plate (the last drops of sauce are always delicious with the greens), could do as well. The *Savoureux* is a substantial but rather less rich than usual chocolate cake. It is fragrant with cinnamon and kirsch and the flavor of hazelnuts, which all blend rather subtly with the chocolate and will be welcome after the rich flavors of the meal. It is certainly difficult to find a wine that is compatible with chocolate, and even for a festive dinner I would hesitate to serve champagne with the *Savoureux*. I know that in my house I would continue pouring red wine—which my husband Jean agrees is wonderful with chocolate—most likely a fine old Bordeaux from Margaux (the wine I prefer of all French wines); or it could be one of the beautiful Private Reserve Cabernets from Beaulieu made in the late sixties—a wine that is, I believe, one of the most noble from California.

Avocats en aspic

For 6:

2 egg whites
1 quart (1 L) richly flavored
   chicken broth, thoroughly
   degreased
1 tablespoon chopped fresh
   tarragon or 1 teaspoon dried
1½ packages unflavored gelatin
¼ cup (½ dL) port or Madeira
Salt and freshly ground pepper

3 large, ripe avocados
Juice of 1 lemon
½ recipe *nouvelle sauce verte,*
   page 217, made with tarragon
2 hard-boiled eggs, peeled
1 hard-boiled egg, peeled and
   pressed through a sieve into
   mimosa
Sprigs of fresh herbs

Recommended equipment: 6 pretty individual glass bowls or soup plates, of about 1⅓ cups (3¼ dL) capacity; a food processor equipped with the metal blade (or an electric mixer)

Break up the egg whites roughly with a whisk and beat in ½ cup (1 dL) of the broth. Then stir the egg whites into the remaining stock. Add the tarragon, pour into a saucepan, and bring to a simmer over medium-low heat. Allow to simmer very gently for 4 or 5 minutes more, then ladle carefully through a fine sieve lined with cheesecloth and set over a bowl, disturbing the egg whites as little as possible. You should have about 3 cups (¾ L) of clarified broth.

Sprinkle the gelatin over the port or Madeira and allow it to soften for a minute or two. Stir into the clear broth, return the liquid to a clean saucepan, and stir over heat until it nears the simmer and the gelatin is dissolved. Season carefully, then set aside at room temperature to cool (or, if you are in a hurry, stir in a metal bowl set over ice water; it should not set).

Slice the avocados in half and remove their pits. Peel, set in a bowl, and sprinkle with the lemon juice to prevent discoloring. Prepare the *sauce verte* in a food processor as directed, then beat in half of the avocados, along with the 2 hard-boiled eggs and ⅓ cup (¾ dL) of the cooled aspic. The sauce should be very smooth. Correct the seasoning, turn into a bowl, and set in the refrigerator to firm up. (If you are working by hand or with an electric mixer, make the *sauce verte* in a mixing bowl, as in the recipe; mash the avocados fine with a fork, then beat them into the sauce, along with the hard-boiled eggs pressed through a sieve.)

Cut the remaining avocado halves into thin slices, but so that they keep their shape. Divide the avocado mayonnaise among the six bowls, spreading it into a smooth layer, then arrange a layer of the sliced avocados over it, fanning them out slightly if you wish. Ladle the cool aspic into the bowls and refrigerate until ready to serve. Garnish with the herbs and with the *mimosa*.

Canards au citron et au whiskey

DUCKS WITH LEMON AND WHISKEY SAUCE

For 6:

3 ducks, 4 pounds (1800 g)
   each, with the neck and
   giblets
½ cup (1 dL) peanut oil
2 medium-sized carrots and
   onions, peeled and sliced
2 tablespoons flour
3 cups (¾ L) dry white
   vermouth
Bouquet garni—parsley, fresh
   or dried thyme, bay leaf

3 lemons
⅔ cup (1½ dL) bourbon
¼ cup (50 g) granulated sugar
3 tablespoons good wine
   vinegar
1½ teaspoons salt
Freshly ground pepper
Lemon juice
4 tablespoons (60 g) butter
Sprigs of watercress

Recommended equipment: A 6- to 8-quart (6–8 L) ovenproof casserole with a lid

Pull away all of the extraneous fat from both ends of the ducks and cut them up, removing the legs and thighs in one piece and the whole breast; refrigerate the meat until you are ready to cook it. Reserve the wings, necks, and backs for the braising liquid; if you have the livers, keep them for another use.

To make the *fond brun* (basic brown sauce), heat 3 tablespoons of the oil in the casserole and add the sliced carrots and onions, with all the bones and the giblets from the ducks, then set the pan in a 450°F (230°C) oven for 30 to 40 minutes to brown, stirring from time to time. When the contents of the pan have nicely browned, sprinkle on the flour and set the casserole back in the oven for another 5 to 10 minutes, stirring once or twice to help the flour brown evenly. Set the casserole on top of the stove, stir in the vermouth and about 3 quarts (3 L) of water, add the *bouquet garni,* and bring the liquid to a boil, stirring and scraping the bottom of the pan to deglaze it thoroughly. Allow to simmer gently over low heat for 2 to 3 hours, skimming it occasionally of any fat and scum and adding any extra water as needed to cover the ingredients. When it seems you have extracted the most good from the bones, strain through a colander, pressing down on the vegetables with a wooden spoon to extract the last drops of flavor. You may degrease the sauce right away, but it will be much easier if you refrigerate it for a few hours and then spoon away the fat from the surface when it has congealed. Once degreased, the sauce is ready and can wait in the refrigerator for a day or two.

Pat the duck legs and thighs dry with a paper towel. In the casserole heat the remaining 5 tablespoons of oil and brown the pieces of duck on all sides, in two lots if necessary, taking care not to crowd the pan. When the meat is all browned, remove it from the pan and pour off the fat. Return the pieces of duck to the casserole, add about half of the prepared brown sauce to the pan, and season it lightly, bringing it to a boil over high heat. Lay a piece of waxed paper or baking parchment over the pieces of duck, cover with the lid, and set the casserole in a 400°F (205°C) oven for 40 to 45 minutes. Turn the meat once during its cooking. The duck is done when the meat begins to shrink slightly from the bone and the juices from a prick in the thigh are beginning to run clear.

While the duck is cooking, begin the flavoring for the sauce. With a vegetable peeler remove the zest from the lemons in neat strips and cut them into fine *julienne* (very thin strips). Cover the peel with water in a small saucepan and boil for about 15 minutes, or until tender; set the peel aside to drain. In a large saucepan, warm the bourbon, then set it alight and allow it to flame gently over low heat for 2 or 3 minutes. Pour in the remaining brown sauce and add all but a few strands of the blanched lemon zest. While the sauce simmers slowly, bring the sugar and vinegar to a boil, *without stirring,* in a small saucepan and cook until it is a rich brown caramel. Off heat, add first drops and then several tablespoons of the simmering sauce, watching out for splatters from the hot sugar. Return the caramel briefly to high heat, swirling to dissolve it thoroughly, then pour the liquid back into the sauce, which can continue simmering gently until the braising duck is ready.

When the legs and thighs are done, pour the braising liquid into a bowl or glass measure and degrease it thoroughly; then add to the simmering sauce. Set the pieces of cooked duck aside in the covered casserole. Boil the sauce more rapidly now, with the saucepan set slightly on the side of the burner to allow you to skim away the fat and scum that will accumulate on the surface. You will want to have, by the time the sauce is reduced, about 2 cups ($\frac{1}{2}$ L). When the flavors and consistency of the sauce seem concentrated to the right point, season with the salt and pepper and add lemon juice, a tablespoon at a time; it should be slightly tart. Pour the sauce back over the pieces of duck, which may now wait at room temperature for an hour or two or overnight in the refrigerator. Be sure to return the casserole to room temperature before rewarming it.

Thirty minutes before serving, bring the duck in its sauce to a simmer on top of the stove. Heat the oven to 450°F (230°C) and roast the duck breasts in a shallow pan in the hot oven for 15 to 18 minutes; the meat should just be medium-rare. Set the breasts aside briefly until they are cool enough to handle, then remove the skin and discard it. Bone the breast meat, carve into thin slices, season with salt and pepper. Rewarm in the turned-off oven while you arrange the legs and thighs on a hot platter. Off heat, swirl the 4 tablespoons (60 g) butter into the hot sauce and correct the seasoning. Place slices of the breast meat over each piece of leg or thigh, pour on a bit of the sauce, and garnish with the watercress and the reserved lemon peel. Pass the remaining sauce in a sauceboat.

Les zéphyrs de pommes de terre

INDIVIDUAL POTATO MOUSSELINES

For 6:

1½ pounds (675 g) boiling
  potatoes
16 tablespoons (225 g) unsalted
  butter, at room temperature
1 whole egg plus 2 extra egg
  yolks

1½ teaspoons salt
Freshly ground pepper
Freshly grated nutmeg
1 teaspoon finely chopped
  fresh parsley

Recommended equipment: Six ⅔-cup (1½ dL) ovenproof dishes— metal baba molds, porcelain or glass custard cups; a food mill

Wash the potatoes, prick them all over with a fork, set them in a shallow ovenproof dish, and bake at 450°F (230°C) for 30 to 40 minutes, or until they are very tender. Spread the sides of the molds evenly with butter, and line the bottoms with rounds of buttered waxed paper.

Allow the potatoes to cool briefly, then peel them and put through the medium disk of a food mill to purée. Beat in the butter, and when well blended, stir in the egg yolks and whole egg, and the seasonings. Spoon the mixture into the prepared molds, which can wait for 2 or 3 hours at room temperature.

To finish the *mousselines,* set them in a flat oven dish and bake at 400°F (205°C) for 15 to 18 minutes, until they have puffed slightly and are just set; they should remain rather soft. The potato molds may be kept in a warm place for up to an hour, and then reheated again briefly in the oven. Unmold, remove the waxed paper, and serve sprinkled with the chopped parsley.

※

Le Savoureux

CHOCOLATE HAZELNUT GÉNOISE WITH
CINNAMON AND KIRSCH

For an 8-inch (20 cm) cake serving 6 to 8:

For the *génoise:*

3 oz (85 g) semisweet chocolate, broken into bits
½ teaspoon cinnamon
3 tablespoons water
2 ounces (60 g) hazelnuts

6 tablespoons granulated sugar
3 eggs, separated
¼ c (30 g) potato starch
Pinch of salt

For the *crème au chocolat* (chocolate butter cream):

6 ounces (170 g) semisweet chocolate, broken into bits
4 tablespoons water
½ teaspoon cinnamon
2 eggs, separated
8 tablespoons (115 g) cold unsalted butter

Pinch of salt
¼ cup (50 g) granulated sugar
¼ cup (½ dL) imported kirsch or Cognac
A dozen or so toasted hazelnuts, split in half

Recommended equipment: An 8-inch (20 cm) cake pan

Butter the sides of the cake pan well and line the bottom with a piece of buttered waxed paper.

Place the chocolate, cinnamon, and water in a heavy-bottomed saucepan over low heat and allow the chocolate to melt, stirring occasionally until it is smooth.

While the chocolate melts, pulverize the hazelnuts in a food processor (or in a blender). In a mixing bowl, gradually beat 3 tablespoons of the sugar into the egg yolks, working them until they have thickened and are pale in color. Stir the hazelnuts and potato starch into the egg mixture, and then the warm chocolate.

Beat the egg whites with a pinch of salt until they form soft peaks; sprinkle on the remaining 3 tablespoons sugar and continue beating until stiff peaks are formed. Delicately fold the chocolate and hazelnut mixture into the beaten whites and turn the batter into the prepared pan. Bake the cake in a 350°F (180°C) oven for 18 to 20 minutes, until it is just set and the sides of the cake are beginning to pull away from the sides of the pan (do not overcook the cake or it will be dry).

Allow the cake to cool on a rack for at least 10 minutes before unmolding it to finish cooling on the rack.

For the *crème au chocolat,* melt the chocolate with the water and cinnamon. When it is smooth, remove the pan from the heat and stir in the egg yolks, one at a time. Return the pan to low heat and stir continuously for 1 or 2 minutes, to warm the egg yolks lightly and thicken the chocolate. Off heat again, stir in the butter, a tablespoon at a time.

Beat the egg whites with the pinch of salt and then the sugar, to form a light meringue, as directed above. Fold the warm chocolate mixture into the meringue and set the cream in the refrigerator or freezer until it is set.

When the cake is completely cool, slice it in half horizontally, using a serrated knife, and sprinkle the cut surfaces with the brandy. Assemble the cake, filling the center with a generous layer of butter cream, and allowing it to firm up in the refrigerator before spreading the top and sides of the cake with the remaining *crème*. Garnish with the hazelnuts.

The cake will keep very well for 2 or 3 days in the refrigerator, where it should remain until 10 minutes before serving.

Un déjeuner bien élaboré

A FESTIVE LUNCH FOR 6

Les oeufs sur mignons de paillasson
EGGS ON POTATO CANAPÉS
WITH LEEK CREAM

vin blanc d'Alsace—Riesling/Joseph Phelps
Johannisberg Riesling

Poulet en roulade
BONED AND ROLLED CHICKEN STUFFED
WITH MUSHROOMS AND EGGPLANT

Salade verte
MIXED GREEN SALAD

Tarte aux pommes Mirliton pour John
CARAMELIZED APPLE TART WITH
ALMOND CUSTARD-CREAM

vin rouge de Touraine—
Chinon/Joseph Heitz Grignolino

Un déjeuner bien élaboré

A FESTIVE LUNCH FOR 6

Here is an attractive lunch composed of distinctive dishes that need a certain care to succeed. The first course combines fried or poached eggs with crisp potato canapés, delicately masked with leeks in cream. To shorten the procedure you could replace the *mignons* by a simple toasted bread canapé, but I do think the potato is more interesting. To simplify your work, the potato canapés and the leek cream can be done ahead of time, with only the eggs needing to be cooked at the last minute—and if you decide to use poached eggs (as noted at the end of the recipe), then everything can be done in advance and reheated.

The *poulet en roulade* is a simplified ballotine I have prepared for students and friends in recent years, and always with great success. It is a dish involving several steps: the complete boning of a chicken (only the drumsticks are left), the preparation of a tasty stuffing with puréed eggplant and mushrooms, the garnishing and rolling of the chicken into a plump sausage shape, and, finally, the braising. The chicken is a very versatile dish—the stuffing given here is only one idea; any nice mixture, with enough body to hold inside the chicken when you roll it, can do as well. One of my favorite variations is with grated and sautéed zucchini mixed with a little cream cheese or creamy goat cheese, plenty of fresh herbs, and some garlic—in fact, very similar to the stuffing for the veal shoulder on page 183. The chicken is also a dish to do two or three days ahead of time, and you can confront the task in stages: bone the chicken one day, roll it and braise it the next. It is fun, too, to carry along on a picnic; the two drumsticks, discreetly crossed, make a neat handle when slicing the chicken. I must say that the chicken is really best eaten cold, when it slices neatly and the stuffing can hold its shape; also, I think the flavors are more enjoyable when they have rested for a while. With the dish nothing more is needed than a green salad in a light vinaigrette (not too acid, because of the wine).

The *Mirliton* is, quite simply, one of the best desserts in this book—an apple tart that will help, I hope, restore the rather bruised reputation of this most traditional of French desserts. Many apple tarts in France are *not* good, if the people making them don't care. But when well done, apples and pastry can be one of the most beautiful tastes at the end of a meal. For the *Mirliton,* dedicated to my dear editor John Ferrone, who loves fine apple desserts, I have looked for something a little new, and so begin with a tart shell made with *pâte sublime*— my latest formula for a delicate sweet pastry—which is prebaked and then painted with apricot glaze. As for the apples, they are thrown into a hot caramel made with butter and sugar, cooked briefly, and then turned onto the pastry to finish cooking with a delicate custard made with cream and almonds—the *crème Mirliton,* from which the dessert takes its name. Certain elements of the dessert can be prepared in advance: the pastry can be molded in the pan and prebaked; the almond cream can be mixed and refrigerated. But the tart itself should be eaten while still tepid from the oven, to have the most pleasure from its tender pastry and soft custard.

Les oeufs sur mignons de paillasson
EGGS ON POTATO CANAPÉS
WITH LEEK CREAM

For 6:

For the *coulis de poireaux* (leeks stewed with white wine and cream):

½ pound (225 g) leeks, trimmed
  of most of the tough or dirty
  green and well washed
4 tablespoons (60 g) butter
3 tablespoons cooking oil
1 cup (¼ L) dry white wine

¾ teaspoon salt
Freshly ground pepper
3 ounces (85 g) boiled ham,
  minced
½ cup (1 dL) heavy cream

For the *mignons de paillasson* (potato canapés):

1½ pounds (675 g) boiling
  potatoes, peeled
2 tablespoons cooking oil

4 tablespoons (60 g) butter, more
  if necessary
1 teaspoon salt
Freshly ground pepper

For the eggs:

6 large eggs
⅔ cup (1½ dL) peanut oil
  (optional)

½ teaspoon salt
Freshly ground pepper

Recommended equipment: A 12-inch (30 cm) nonstick skillet with a lid

Chop the white and tender green of the leeks fine with a knife, and cook over low heat with the butter and oil in the covered skillet for

8 to 10 minutes, stirring occasionally. Add the white wine and season-ings and allow the mixture to continue simmering, uncovered, for another 15 to 18 minutes. When the leeks are very tender, stir in the ham and heavy cream and reduce over medium heat until the sauce thickens slightly. Correct the seasoning; scrape the *coulis* into a sauce-pan and set aside.

Grate the potatoes coarsely in a food processor or with a hand grater. Wash them in two or three changes of cold water. If they are not to be used immediately, keep immersed in a bowl of cold water. Drain and pat thoroughly dry in a towel. In the washed nonstick skillet, heat the oil and butter and arrange the potatoes in 6 neat stacks. If you are using a smaller skillet, you may want to do them in two batches, or else use a second skillet. Brown over medium-low heat for 10 to 15 minutes on each side, adding more butter if necessary, and gradually pressing the potatoes down with a wooden or metal spatula to form fairly compact canapés. Salt and pepper about halfway through the cooking. When a crisp golden brown, remove to a platter and keep warm; at the last minute they should be crisped again in the skillet with a bit of butter.

Stir the leek mixture over medium heat to warm it through and keep it warm over low heat while you cook the eggs. Either fry them in peanut oil, basting them with the hot oil as they cook or poach them, according to your taste. When done, arrange on the hot potato canapés and season. Spoon the leek-cream sauce over all. Garnish with a small bouquet of parsley, if you wish.

X

Poulet en roulade

BONED AND ROLLED CHICKEN STUFFED
WITH MUSHROOMS AND EGGPLANT

For 6:

1 fresh chicken, 4 pounds (1800 g), with the giblets and liver

3 to 4 cups (¾–1 L) *unsalted* chicken broth made from the bones

A small eggplant, about ½ pound (225 g)

2 chicken livers

1 tablespoon (15 g) butter

2 tablespoons Cognac

1 tablespoon dry Madeira

½ recipe creamy minced mushrooms, page 219

2 ounces (60 g) stale white bread, crusts removed

Several sprigs of fresh herbs— any combination of basil, parsley, chervil, or chives

3 cloves garlic, peeled

1 egg

Salt and freshly ground pepper

Freshly grated nutmeg

4 to 5 tablespoons cooking oil

2 cups (½ L) dry white wine

Sprigs of fresh herbs or crisp lettuce leaves

1 recipe *nouvelle sauce verte,* page 217

Recommended equipment: A 9- to 10-inch (25 cm) nonstick skillet; a 6- to 8-quart (6–8 L) flameproof casserole with a lid; a food processor equipped with the metal blade

To bone the chicken, remove all the extraneous fat from both ends, remove the wishbone by scraping with a small knife over the V-shaped opening at the neck end of the bird and then pulling out the exposed bone. Lay the chicken breast side down and slit the skin down the center of the back. Working on one side, peel away the leg and thigh, the wing, and the whole breast in one piece along with the skin, continuing down to the tip of the breast bone (if you pierce the skin, this can be mended later on). Repeat the boning operation on the other side of the chicken. Remove the carcass by cutting and scraping with your knife along the length of the breast-bone ridge.

Lay the chicken flat on your working surface. Cut away the wings, and bone out the thigh bones and any tough cartilage near the joint: the leg, or drumstick, is the only bone remaining. The chicken is now ready to receive its stuffing; it can be wrapped in plastic wrap and refrigerated for a day before it is stuffed. Make the broth, using the carcass, bones, and giblets of the chicken. *Be sure not to salt.* Save the liver, and add to the other livers.

To make the stuffing, prick the skin of the eggplant all over with a fork and bake it in a 375°F (190°C) oven for 30 to 40 minutes, until it is very tender. Remove and set aside to cool.

While the eggplant bakes pick over the livers, removing any stringy bits. Melt the butter in the skillet over medium-low heat and sauté the livers gently, tossing or stirring them for 1 to 2 minutes. Pour on the Cognac and Madeira and set alight, shaking the pan to help burn off the alcohol. Season the livers lightly and remove from the pan. Cook the mushrooms as directed (their final chopping will come later on).

When the eggplant has cooled, cut it in half and scoop out the flesh, scraping away the seeds. Grind the bread in a food processor into fairly fine crumbs, then add the herbs and garlic and chop them fine. Add the livers, mushrooms, eggplant, egg, 1 teaspoon salt, pepper, and nutmeg, and blend the stuffing for a few seconds (the mushrooms and livers should be finely chopped but not a purée). Taste carefully for seasoning. (If you are working by hand, grate the bread, chop the herbs, garlic, livers, mushrooms, and eggplant separately, then add the ingredients to a mixing bowl and blend them with the egg and seasoning.) The stuffing may now be turned into a bowl, covered with plastic wrap and refrigerated for up to a day before proceeding with the recipe.

Lay the chicken skin side down, salt and pepper the meat, then spread a ¼-inch (⅔ cm) layer of stuffing over it, tucking a little extra stuffing into the drumstick pocket and leaving a border of about ½ inch (1¼ cm) around the edge of the chicken. Bring the sides together to enclose the stuffing. Using needle and thread, sew the chicken tightly shut, making a seam down the center. Fold it in half; then roll it up, thighs neatly crossed, in a single layer of cheesecloth. Twist and tie the ends of the cheesecloth with string, then tie at intervals along the length of the chicken to shape it like a plump sausage. Heat the oil in the casserole set over medium-high heat, then brown the chicken on all sides. It will take on color very well through the cheesecloth.

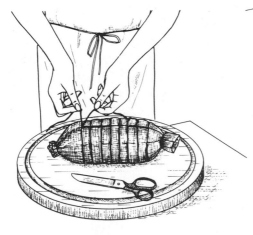

Pour off the fat from the pan, then add the wine, and simmer for 2 minutes. Pour in the broth to come about one-third of the way up the sides of the chicken. Bring to a simmer on top of the stove. Then place a piece of waxed paper or baking parchment on the surface of the chicken, cover the casserole, and cook in a 375°F (190°C) oven for 45 minutes, turning the bird once or twice.

Remove from the oven and allow the chicken to cool in its braising liquid. Then wrap the chicken in foil and refrigerate. Degrease the broth and boil it in a saucepan until it has reduced to about ½ cup (1 dL) and is syrupy. Set aside to cool. The chicken and the glaze may be kept in the refrigerator for a day or two before finishing the dish.

When the chicken is cold, remove the string, cheesecloth, and thread. Cut into nice ¼-inch (⅔ cm) slices, and arrange attractively on a serving platter, along with the drumsticks. Paint the chicken with several coats of the glaze (melt it over low heat if it has set), and add whatever green garnish you have chosen. Serve with the *sauce verte*.

Tarte aux pommes Mirliton pour John

CARAMELIZED APPLE TART WITH

ALMOND CUSTARD-CREAM

For a 9- to 10-inch (23–25 cm) tart serving 6 to 8:

12 ounces (340 g) *pâte sublime,*
   page 213
⅓ cup (¾ dL) apricot jam
1 pound (450 g) good eating
   apples—Golden Delicious,
   pippin, Granny Smith, etc.
⅓ cup (65 g) granulated sugar
4 tablespoons (60 g) unsalted
   butter

1 teaspoon lemon juice
⅓ cup (70 g) blanched almonds
1 egg
¼ cup (30 g) powdered sugar,
   sifted
⅓ cup (¾ dL) heavy cream
½ teaspoon vanilla extract or 2
   tablespoons dark rum

Recommended equipment: A 9- to 10-inch (23–25 cm) false-bottomed tart tin

Make the pastry and chill it. Roll out about ⅛ inch (⅓ cm) thick on a lightly floured surface into a circle slightly larger than the tart tin, lifting and sliding the dough frequently to prevent it from sticking and also to feel it for thickness. Fit the dough into the tart tin, pushing it down around the sides to make them a little thicker. Press the rolling pin over the tin to trim away the extra dough, and press the pastry up the sides to extend slightly above the rim. Prick the bottom all over with a fork, and set the pastry-lined tin into the freezer to firm up for at least 10 to 15 minutes.

In the meantime, melt the jam over heat in a small saucepan, stirring until it is liquid, then set aside to cool.

When the pastry is firm, bake in a 450°F (230°C) oven for 5 to 6 minutes, then lower the heat to 375°F (190°C) and bake for an additional 4 to 5 minutes to precook. If it puffs during baking, prick with a fork. Remove from the oven and paint with half of the apricot glaze.

Peel and core the apples and cut them into ½-inch (1⅓ cm) dice. Place the granulated sugar, butter, and lemon juice in a heavy-bottomed saucepan and set it over medium-high heat. Stir the mixture occasionally as it melts and begins to caramelize; it should cook to a nice golden brown, which will take about 3 to 4 minutes. Add the apples to the pan and stir them over heat for 4 to 5 minutes.

While the apples cook, prepare the custard. Pulverize the almonds to a fine powder in a food processor or in an electric blender. Then beat in the egg, powdered sugar, cream, and the vanilla or rum. Spread the hot apples in the tart shell in an even layer. Pour in the custard. Bake for 20 minutes, until the custard is just set. Allow to cool on a rack for 10 to 15 minutes before unmolding onto a serving dish. It is best served warm, and within an hour or two of baking. If you must bake it several hours ahead, it can be rewarmed in a 300°F (150°C) oven for 10 to 15 minutes. Before serving, brush with the remaining apricot glaze, slightly rewarmed if necessary.

Une réception en vogue

A FASHIONABLE SUPPER PARTY FOR 12

Beurre de saumon
MOLDED PÂTÉ OF FRESH AND
SMOKED SALMON

Lapin et deux volailles en gelée
RABBIT AND FOWL IN VEGETABLE ASPIC

Salade d'endives
BELGIAN ENDIVE VINAIGRETTE

Charlotte en rosaces
APRICOT BAVARIAN CREAM MOLDED
IN SPONGE CAKE

*tout au Champagne—
blanc de blancs "cremant"/Robert Mondavi Brut
(Napa Valley sparkling white wine)*
or
*vin blanc de Bourgogne—
Meursault/Château Montelena Pinot
Chardonnay*

Une réception en vogue

A FASHIONABLE SUPPER PARTY FOR 12

This is an elegant menu from start to finish, beginning with a luxurious molded salmon pâté, followed by a colorful rabbit and fowl in aspic, and finishing with a Bavarian cream, airy and blushing with apricot. It is a supper party or buffet menu for twelve chic friends, calling for much champagne. Because all of the dishes are cold, they can easily be readied ahead of time, and the cook in the house will be free to join the party.

I have frequently enjoyed combining smoked salmon with fresh, and in the *beurre de saumon* the idea receives an extravagant interpretation in a molded dish that can be served in several ways: in thin slices, accompanied by toast; spooned into pretty oval shapes; or on canapés, as an hors-d'oeuvre. I recently made this pâté for a Christmas Eve supper, and as the fresh French salmon was quite exorbitant, I bought some frozen Pacific Coast salmon for one-fourth the price! It was very, very good, and once it was puréed one would never have known the difference. So you can use some frozen salmon for this dish, or any other delicate fish for that matter—trout, for instance—but of course, the beauty of salmon is also in its color.

The *lapin et deux volailles en gelée* has been a favorite recipe for twenty-five years. The simmering of the various meats with aromatic vegetables and slices of lemon becomes a light and refreshing dish in jelly that will keep very well for two or three days before serving— as will the salmon dish. On the day of your party, you have only to unmold the dish and garnish it. The ingredients can be varied—it can be done only with chicken, for instance. The clarifying of the aspic takes extra work and is optional, but if you do it, you will have a handsomer dish. Something to note is that there is no browning of any of the meat in the dish. The pieces are simply packed into the pan, along with the vegetables, and then covered with a good stock, making it relatively uncomplicated to do.

A Bavarian cream is always a spectacular way to finish a special dinner, and for me the best formula for this dessert is the one I have used over the years, where beaten egg whites lighten a *crème anglaise* bound with gelatin, which is then enriched with a little beaten cream. For the dessert to have a delicate, melting quality on the tongue, it must not contain too much gelatin, but at the same time it should have enough to give it body. Recently, for a cooking class in Venice, Michael and I had to work with an unfamiliar kind of gelatin, which was not strong enough, and our unmolded dessert began to sink like Venice itself! But a good cook knows how to recover, and it is an easy matter to spoon a too-soft Bavarian into individual *coupes*.

In any event, an impressive twist to a Bavarian cream—and something that is quite fashionable now with caterers and pastry chefs all over—is to mold the dessert inside slices of jelly roll spread with a fruit glaze. When unmolded, the sponge-cake casing is brushed with more of the glaze, to present a gleaming appearance reminiscent of roses, so I have titled my version of this dessert *charlotte en rosaces*. For the flavoring Michael and I have worked out a tart and unusual *bavarois* made with a purée of dried apricots, a delicious fruit flavor that is practical because it is available year round. Of course, the flavor can be varied—by using a purée of sweet peaches in the summer, for example, or by using the more classic formula of orange and vanilla. The glaze, too, can be changed to raspberry, red-currant, or any other; and the liqueur, to rum or kirsch. To simplify the dessert, you could easily omit the sponge cake and serve only the molded Bavarian cream, which on its own is splendid.

Beurre de saumon

MOLDED PÂTÉ OF FRESH AND SMOKED SALMON

For 12:

1 cup (¼ L) dry white wine
1 tablespoon chopped fresh
   tarragon or 1 teaspoon dried
Freshly ground pepper
2 teaspoons chopped fresh dill or
   ¼ teaspoon dried (optional)
1 pound (450 g) fresh or frozen
   boneless salmon (1½ pounds
   [675 g] with the bones and
   skin), cut into 3 or 4 pieces

2 to 3 tablespoons olive oil
1 clove garlic, peeled and minced
½ pound (225 g) good-quality
   smoked salmon—in 1 thick
   slice, if possible
20 tablespoons (2½ sticks;
   285 g) unsalted butter
3 tablespoons vodka

Recommended equipment: A 1-quart (1 L) plain round or rectangular metal mold; a 1-quart (1 L) stainless steel saucepan (or other suitable pan, but *not* aluminum); a food processor equipped with the metal blade

In the saucepan, bring the wine, tarragon, some pepper, and the optional dill to a simmer. After the alcohol has evaporated for a minute or two, poach the fresh or thawed salmon: depending on the thickness of the pieces, it will probably take about 1 minute. The fish should remain rosy and a little creamy in the middle; when it is done, remove it to a rack or plate to cool. Rapidly reduce the poaching liquid to 2 or 3 tablespoons and set aside.

    In a medium-sized skillet, warm the olive oil, then add the minced garlic and cook it gently for about 1 minute. Add the smoked salmon and sauté 30 seconds on each side. Remove from the pan and blot away the oil with paper towels. Purée the fresh and smoked salmon in the food processor, then beat in the wine reduction, butter, and vodka and correct the seasoning (little or no salt will be needed). Pack the pâté mixture into the mold, cover with plastic wrap and chill for at least 3 to 4 hours. It will keep easily in the refrigerator for several days and also freezes nicely.

If using the pâté as a canapé spread, take a small, sharp knife and simply spread it directly from the mold onto thin slices of rye bread, trimmed of their crusts and cut, if you wish, into attractive shapes. Or serve unmolded and cut into thin slices about ¼ inch (⅔ cm) thick, along with toasted *pain de mie au lait* (see page 215). To serve *en coquilles,* spoon out little shell shapes in an attractive mound on a plate. This is done with two spoons dipped in hot water, one scooping out the pâté neatly and compactly, and the other nudging it out of the spoon onto the plate. The pâté is very pretty and also delicious when garnished with bits of *olives niçoises,* the tiny black olives from the south of France.

Lapin et deux volailles en gelée

RABBIT AND FOWL IN VEGETABLE ASPIC

For 12:

1 rabbit, 2½ to 3 pounds (1350 g), the saddle cut into 1-inch (2½ cm) sections, the rest cut into serving pieces

1 4-pound (1800 g) fresh chicken, cut into serving pieces, or 3 pounds (1350 g) chicken legs, thighs and breasts

2 pigeons or Cornish game hens, about 1 pound (450 g) each, split in half

1 tablespoon coriander seeds, coarsely crushed

1 teaspoon peppercorns, coarsely crushed

⅓ cup (¾ dL) olive oil

3 medium carrots and 2 medium onions, peeled and thinly sliced

1 pound (450 g) celery root, peeled, cut into eighths and sliced ¼-inch (⅔ cm) thick or if not in season, sliced stalk celery

2 red or green bell peppers,
   seeded and cut into thin
   strips
Salt
6 unpeeled cloves of garlic
3 or 4 lemons, cut into round
   slices about ⅛-inch (⅓ cm)
   thick
Bouquet garni—parsley, fresh
   or dried thyme, bay leaf

⅓ cup (¾ dL) good wine
   vinegar
2 cups (½ L) dry white wine
3 cups (¾ L) stock made from
   the carcasses of the rabbit and
   chicken or 3 cups (¾ L)
   chicken stock
1 package unflavored gelatin
1 tablespoon chopped parsley
Crisp lettuce leaves or sprigs of
   watercress

Recommended equipment: A 6- to 8-quart (6–8 L) enameled cast-iron (or plain cast-iron) oven casserole with a lid; a large dish about 15 inches (38 cm) long, 10 inches (25 cm) wide, and 3 inches (8 cm) deep for molding the aspic

Rub the rabbit and fowl with the coriander and peppercorns; set aside.

In the casserole, heat the olive oil. Add the onions and cook them over medium heat for 2 or 3 minutes, then add the carrots and celery root. Cook the vegetables for 8 to 10 minutes, stirring occasionally, until they begin to be tender. Add the strips of bell pepper and continue cooking for another 5 minutes or so. Remove the casserole from the heat; season lightly.

Spoon most of the vegetables out of the casserole, leaving only an even layer on the bottom. Lay the rabbit meat and dark chicken meat neatly over the vegetables, add 1 or 2 cloves of garlic, and insert some of the lemon slices between the pieces of meat. Spread on another layer of vegetables, and over them arrange the white pieces of chicken meat with more garlic and lemon. Continue with the vegetables, the pieces of pigeon or game hen, garlic and lemon. Finish with a layer of vegetables. Top with the *bouquet garni*.

Pour on the vinegar, stock, and white wine. The contents of the pan should just be covered; add a little extra stock or wine, if necessary. Set the casserole over medium heat and bring the liquid to a simmer. Place a piece of waxed paper or baking parchment directly on the surface of the vegetables, cover and cook in a 375°F (190°C) oven for 1 hour, or until all of the meat is tender.

When the dish is done, remove it to room temperature and allow the meat to rest in the liquid for 15 to 20 minutes. Then use a slotted skimmer to lift the meat and vegetables into a shallow tray or large bowl to cool. Remove all of the pieces of meat from the vegetables. Carefully skin and bone the chicken thighs and breasts, keeping as much of the meat intact as possible. Skin the drumsticks. Then bone the rabbit and other poultry. Season the meat lightly, if necessary. Strain the cooking liquid through a fine sieve into a saucepan. (If you wish you can refrigerate the meat and the cooking liquid at this point and proceed with the recipe the next day.) Degrease the stock thoroughly. Sprinkle the gelatin over 3 or 4 tablespoons of water in a small cup and allow it to soften. Stir into the cooking liquid (warmed slightly if it is cold), and continue stirring over medium heat until the gelatin is thoroughly dissolved. Correct the seasoning, and set it aside to cool; you should have about 4 cups (1 L).

In the dish for molding make an attractive pattern with some of the vegetables and slices of lemon; sprinkle on the parsley and spoon in a shallow layer of the cooled aspic. Set in the refrigerator briefly to partially set. Next, arrange the boneless pieces of meat in an even layer, and finish with the last of the vegetables, packing them in firmly. Pour in the remaining aspic. Set the dish in the refrigerator for at least 2 hours before serving, to allow the aspic to set. Once molded, the dish can easily wait for a day or two.

To serve, dip briefly in hot water, then run a flexible metal spatula around the edges of the dish, place a serving platter over it, and invert the two, using a sharp downward motion to help dislodge the aspic. If the dish doesn't unmold at first, lift one edge and insert the spatula along the side to break its seal. Garnish with the lettuce or watercress and serve, spooning up some of the vegetables with each piece of meat.

Charlotte en rosaces

APRICOT BAVARIAN CREAM MOLDED
IN SPONGE CAKE

For 10 to 12:

For the jelly roll:

3 eggs, separated
½ cup (100 g) granulated sugar
½ teaspoon vanilla extract
½ cup (70 g) all-purpose flour

Pinch of salt
2 to 3 tablespoons orange liqueur
   or Benedictine
¾ cup (1¾ dL) apricot jam

For the Bavarian cream and glaze:

6 ounces (170 g) dried apricots
3 cubes sugar
1 large orange
4 to 5 tablespoons orange liqueur
   or Benedictine
1½ packages unflavored gelatin
1½ cups (3½ dL) milk

1 vanilla bean, split in half
4 eggs, separated, and 2 extra
   yolks
¾ cup (140 g) granulated sugar
Pinch of salt
⅔ cup (1½ dL) heavy cream
½ cup (1 dL) apricot jam

Recommended equipment: An 11 x 16-inch (28 x 40 cm) rectangular jelly-roll pan; an 8-cup (2 L) metal charlotte mold

Line the jelly-roll pan with foil and butter well. Beat the egg yolks with ¼ cup (50 g) of the sugar until the mixture is fluffy and pale lemon-colored. Stir in the vanilla extract and then the flour. The mixture will be very thick. Beat the egg whites with a pinch of salt until they form soft peaks. Sprinkle on the remaining ¼ cup (50 g) sugar and continue beating until the meringue forms fairly stiff peaks. Stir ⅓ of the beaten whites into the egg-yolk mixture to lighten it, then fold in the remaining meringue. Spread the batter evenly into the prepared pan, using a rubber or metal spatula. Bake in a 375°F (190°C) oven for 12 to 15 minutes, until the cake is a nice golden brown and has pulled away slightly from the sides of the foil.

Remove from the oven and turn out onto a kitchen towel wrung out in cold water. (The dampness creates steam, which prevents the cake from sticking and drying out.) Remove the buttered foil and save it for later. Grasp the length of the towel evenly and roll up the sponge layer in it, to shape it as it cools. While the cake is cooling, liquefy the jam in a small saucepan over moderate heat, stirring until smooth; put it through a fine sieve, then set aside to cool and thicken slightly. Unroll the sponge cake, sprinkle generously with the liqueur, and paint with the apricot glaze. Roll up the cake again, and transfer to the reserved piece of foil. Wrap the foil around the roll, refrigerate until cooled, and then set in the freezer for 10 minutes before slicing.

Simmer the dried apricots in 1 cup (¼ L) water until they are plump and tender. Purée in a food processor or put through the medium disk of a food mill, along with any remaining liquid. Set aside to cool. Rub the sugar cubes over the surface of the orange to extract the oil from the zest. Crush the cubes with a spoon, sprinkling on a few drops of the orange liqueur to help them dissolve, and add the orange sugar to the egg yolks. Squeeze the juice from the orange—you should have about ⅓ cup (¾ dL)—and sprinkle in the gelatin to soften.

Bring the milk, with the vanilla bean, to a simmer in a heavy-bottomed saucepan. Beat the egg yolks with the orange sugar, then gradually add ½ cup (100 g) of the sugar, beating until the mixture thickens slightly and is pale lemon-colored. Beat the hot milk into the egg yolk mixture, pouring slowly at first, then more rapidly as the mixture is warmed through. Pour the mixture back into the warm saucepan and stir it over moderate heat, using a wooden spatula, until the custard has thickened enough to coat the spatula with a light layer. It will foam up slightly in the pan and be hot to the finger, but should not simmer. Off the heat remove the vanilla bean (you can scrape its sticky insides into the custard) and add the orange juice and gelatin mixture, beating it into the custard until well dissolved.

Butter the sides of the mold generously with butter. Cut the cold jelly roll into thin slices, about ¼ inch (⅔ cm) thick, and line the bottom and sides of the mold with a neat and compact layer. Save any scraps or leftover slices for finishing the dessert.

Beat the egg whites with the pinch of salt until they form soft peaks. Sprinkle on the remaining ¼ cup (50 g) sugar, and continue beating the whites until they form stiff peaks. Delicately fold the warm custard mixture into the egg whites. Set the bowl in the refrigerator to chill, folding the mixture from time to time with a rubber spatula so that it begins to set evenly and does not separate. When the mixture is cold but not yet set, beat the cream until it is stiff. Stir, along with 2 tablespoons of the liqueur, into the cool apricot purée, then fold into the chilled custard. Pour into the prepared mold. Trim off any protruding bits of cake, and poke them into the surface of the Bavarian cream. Chill for at least 3 hours, until set, or for up to a day or two.

When ready to serve, warm the apricot jam with the remaining liqueur until it is smooth. Then press it through a fine sieve. Dip the chilled dessert mold into hot water for a few seconds, to warm the buttered sides and allow the dessert to slip out easily. Dry the mold with a towel and invert onto a serving platter. Paint on the tepid glaze. To serve, slice with a serrated knife into wedges.

Menus with Meat

MAIN DISHES:

Aillade d'agneau

Côtes de porc à la Foyot

Palette de veau au paprika

Hamburgers à la provençale

Nougat de boeuf

Gigot anglo-normand à la crème moutardée

Épaule de veau farcie et roulée

Un menu pour amateurs d'ail

A MENU FOR GARLIC ENTHUSIASTS,
FOR 6 TO 8

*Courgettes farcies aux herbes
et au fromage blanc*
STUFFED ZUCCHINI WITH HERBS
AND CREAM CHEESE

Aillade d'agneau
LAMB SHOULDER STEW WITH GARLIC

Gratin de pommes de terre normand
POTATO GRATIN WITH TARRAGON AND CREAM

Glace au macadamia
MACADAMIA NUT ICE CREAM

*Côtes de Provence rouge—
Bandol / David Bruce Cabernet Sauvignon*

Un menu pour amateurs d'ail

A MENU FOR GARLIC ENTHUSIASTS,
FOR 6 TO 8

There are corners of France very dear to me, and this menu contains flavors of three of them—the light entrée dish with *courgettes* is somehow Parisian; the honest and simple lamb dish, Provençal; and of course the potatoes with their tarragon and cream, Normand. Then there is the flavor of a foreign province, far from France but close to my heart—Hawaii, where I first discovered the macadamia nut, used in this menu for an ice cream.

With the stuffed *courgettes* you have a first course that is tasty and green at the same time, and yet not too filling to precede the hearty lamb. I have included hard-boiled eggs as well as some cream cheese to give a pleasing texture to the squash stuffing, which in this version contains a purée of the scooped-out zucchini and onions. As for the lamb stew, this was first inspired by my friend Richard Olney, a cook with ingenious ideas, who braises his lamb shanks in a very large quantity of garlic that later becomes the sauce. My idea was to choose a cut of lamb that would be elegant for a dinner party and also easy to eat only with a fork (always useful for a buffet). The *aillade,* then, makes use of a shoulder of lamb, one of the nicest cuts of that animal, I think, as it has a rich flavor and rather gelatinous quality that makes it especially succulent when braised. The cut-up pieces of lamb are cooked in a rich broth with four bulbs (several dozen cloves) of unpeeled garlic, which at the end of the cooking are strained and puréed to bind the sauce with a lovely softened flavor. So don't panic at so much garlic; when it is properly cooked it is never overpowering. The *aillade* is a wonderful dish to do ahead and reheat, as it can only gain in flavor when it rests for a while. To accompany the meat I

132

know of no better dish than a potato *gratin,* which in this case is delicately flavored with tarragon rather than with the usual cheese and hint of garlic.

French ice cream is classically made with a custard and not necessarily cream, and the *glace au macadamia* is no exception. Although I am partial to the rich macadamia nut, certainly this dessert could be very good with almonds, or even pecans.

Courgettes farcies aux herbes
et au fromage blanc

STUFFED ZUCCHINI WITH HERBS
AND CREAM CHEESE

For 8:

2½ pounds (1350 g) firm, fresh zucchini

5 tablespoons olive oil

¾ pound (340 g) onions, peeled and minced

1½ teaspoons salt

Freshly ground pepper

5 ounces (140 g) cream cheese, preferably without gum additives

1 cup (¼ L) plus 3 tablespoons sour cream

2 hard-boiled eggs, peeled and chopped

2 raw eggs

1 cup (120 g) stale, coarse white bread crumbs

½ cup (45 g) grated Gruyère cheese

1 tablespoon each freshly chopped parsley and basil

1 teaspoon *herbes de Provence* (see page 220)

¼ cup (25 g) Parmesan cheese

Recommended equipment: 2 large oval gratin dishes

Wash the zucchini and trim the ends. Cut each in half lengthwise. With a teaspoon or grapefruit spoon, scoop out the insides, leaving a ¼-inch (⅔ cm) border. Chop the zucchini flesh fine, and set aside.

133

Blanch the zucchini shells in a large quantity of boiling salted water for 8 to 10 minutes, depending on the quality of the vegetable; it should still be quite tender. Refresh under cold running water and set aside to drain.

Heat the oil in a skillet—nonstick, if possible—and cook the onion over medium-low heat, stirring frequently. After 10 minutes add the chopped zucchini flesh, raise the heat slightly, and continue cooking and stirring for 12 to 15 minutes more. Season the mixture well with some of the salt and a bit of pepper, and put in a food processor or through the fine disk of a food mill to make a fine purée. Then beat in the cream cheese, 3 tablespoons sour cream, the 2 hard-boiled eggs and the 2 raw eggs, the bread, Gruyère, herbs, and salt and pepper.

Oil the gratin dishes lightly. Arrange the zucchini shells snugly in the dishes. Salt and pepper them lightly, then spoon in the stuffing so the shells are quite full. The filled zucchini can wait an hour or two at room temperature.

To finish the dish, bake it in a 375°F (190°C) oven for 18 to 20 minutes, then spread the surface of the stuffing with the 1 cup (¼ L) sour cream mixed with the Parmesan cheese. Return to a 425°F (220°C) oven for 10 minutes, then run briefly under a hot broiler to lightly brown. The zucchini may be kept warm in the turned-off oven for 15 to 20 minutes. Serve from the dish.

Aillade d'agneau

LAMB SHOULDER STEW WITH GARLIC

For 6 to 8:

4 pounds (1800 g) lamb shoulder, boned (reserve bones) and trimmed of gristle and most fat	Freshly ground pepper
	4 heads garlic, crushed to separate the cloves and left unpeeled
3 to 4 tablespoons olive oil	Generous *bouquet garni*—
1 cup (¼ L) dry white wine	parsley, fresh or dried thyme,
2 cups (½ L) good veal or poultry stock	bay leaf
	1 tablespoon finely chopped
1 teaspoon salt	fresh parsley

Recommended equipment: A 6- to 8-quart (6–8 L) plain or enameled cast-iron ovenproof casserole with a lid

Cut the lamb shoulder into 3- to 4-ounce (85–115 g) pieces of approximately the same shape; dry with an absorbent towel. Heat the oil in the casserole over medium heat and brown the pieces of lamb, then the bones, lightly on all sides in a loose, single layer. You will probably need to do this in two batches.

Pour off the fat from the pan, then add a spoonful or so of the wine to deglaze the bottom. Arrange the meat and bones in the pan, salt and pepper lightly, add the cloves of garlic and the *bouquet garni,* and pour on the remaining wine. Bring to a simmer on top of the stove, then add the stock. Return to a simmer, place a piece of waxed paper over the meat and cover. Cook in a 375°F (190°C) oven, turning the pieces once or twice, for 1½ hours to 1 hour 45 minutes; the meat should be very tender but not falling apart.

Transfer the meat to a serving platter and keep warm in the turned-off oven covered with the waxed paper; discard the bones. Remove the cooked garlic from the casserole and purée it through the fine disk of a food mill, to remove its stringy skin. Degrease the cooking liquid thoroughly and, if you feel it is needed, reduce over high heat to concentrate its flavor. Stir in the garlic purée and taste the sauce for seasoning. You should have about 1½ cups (3½ dL). The dish may wait at this point for 20 to 30 minutes. When you are ready to serve, bring the sauce back to a simmer, then pour it over the meat and sprinkle with the chopped parsley.

To prepare the dish several hours or a day ahead, cook the lamb for only 1½ hours, allow it to cool completely in its liquid, then proceed with the finishing of the sauce as described in the recipe. Return the meat and sauce to the casserole and set aside; or, if done the day before, refrigerate (be sure to remove to room temperature at least 1 hour before serving). Reheat the lamb in a 350°F (180°C) oven for 20 to 25 minutes, or until hot through. Serve from the casserole, or on a serving platter, sprinkled with the parsley.

Gratin de pommes de terre normand

POTATO GRATIN WITH TARRAGON AND CREAM

For 6 to 8:

2 pounds (900 g) boiling
 potatoes, peeled
3 cups (¾ L) milk, more if
 necessary
Freshly grated nutmeg

1 teaspoon chopped fresh
 tarragon or ¼ teaspoon dried
2 teaspoons salt
Freshly ground pepper
½ cup (1 dL) heavy cream

Recommended equipment: A 12-inch (30 cm) oval gratin dish

Cut the potatoes into ⅛-inch (⅓ cm) thick slices. Cover them with the milk in a large saucepan and add the nutmeg, tarragon, and seasonings. Bring to a simmer and cook for 4 minutes. Meanwhile, butter the baking dish. Using a slotted spoon, remove the potatoes from the pan and arrange them in an even layer in the buttered dish. Taste the milk carefully for seasoning and pour it over the potatoes, which should be well covered by liquid at all times during cooking. If necessary, add a little extra milk. Bake in a 375°F (190°C) oven for about 25 minutes, until the potatoes are just tender. Pour the cream over them, and return the dish to a 450°F (230°C) oven for 8 to 10 minutes, until the surface is lightly browned; if you wish, run the potatoes briefly under a hot broiler. The dish can be kept warm in the turned-off oven for 30 to 40 minutes or may be completed 1 or 2 hours in advance and reheated in a moderate oven for 10 to 15 minutes, until the gratin is beginning to bubble.

Variation: A l'oseille (With sorrel). Omit the tarragon, and spread the potatoes with a layer of creamed sorrel instead of the heavy cream.

Glace au macadamia

MACADAMIA NUT ICE CREAM

For 6 to 8:

2½ ounces (70 g) unsalted
   macadamia nuts (see page
   14), more if desired
2 cups (½ L) milk
1 whole vanilla bean, split, or 1
   teaspoon vanilla extract

½ c (100 g) plus 2 tablespoons
   granulated sugar
6 egg yolks
3 tablespoons dark rum

Recommended equipment: A food processor fitted with the metal blade (or a blender); an ice-cream maker

Toast the macadamia nuts in a 350°F (180°C) oven for 8 to 10 minutes, or until they are lightly browned. Remove them to room temperature to cool.

Place the milk with the vanilla bean or extract in a heavy-bottomed medium-sized saucepan, and bring it barely to a simmer. Meanwhile, gradually whisk the ½ cup (100 g) of sugar into the yolks, beating until thickened and pale in color. Then whisk the hot milk slowly into the egg mixture, by drops at first and then in a steady stream. Return the mixture to the saucepan, place it over medium-low heat, and stir it steadily, using a wooden spoon or spatula, until the custard thickens slightly and coats the spoon with a light layer—it should be very hot to the finger, but do not allow to simmer. Stir momentarily off heat, to cool the custard slightly; remove the vanilla bean.

Pulverize the macadamia nuts in a food processor (or in two lots in a blender), adding the remaining sugar so the nuts don't turn to a butter. Beat in a few spoonfuls of the warm custard, to lighten the mixture, then turn out into a mixing bowl and stir in the remaining custard along with the rum. Set in the refrigerator to cool completely. Pour into the container of the ice-cream maker and freeze. If you wish, you may then mold the ice cream in a small (1 quart or 1 L) metal mold. Set the ice cream in the freezer until ready to serve.

To serve, either unmold the ice cream and serve in slices, or simply scoop it into dishes. Garnish with a few extra toasted and chopped macadamia nuts, if you wish.

Un simple menu pour un déjeuner

A SIMPLE LUNCH FOR 6

Le céleri-rave rémoulade
GRATED CELERY ROOT WITH
HERB MAYONNAISE

Côtes de porc à la Foyot
GRATINÉED PORK CHOPS WITH ONIONS

Blettes panachées au fromage
LAYERS OF SWISS CHARD WITH CHEESE
(PAGE 34)

Petites crèmes au citron
LEMON CREAMS IN RAMEQUINS

vin rosé naturel du Rhône—
Tavel/Caymus "Oeil de Perdrix"

Un simple menu pour un déjeuner

A SIMPLE LUNCH FOR 6

A platter of raw garden vegetables—*crudités*—can be one of the most colorful and refreshing ways to begin a meal, and certainly it is one of the most French. For lunches at home it is what my husband Jean and I will have most often, and what could be simpler to prepare? During the cool months (in Provence, any really cold weather is quite unusual), we have wonderful tiny *fenouils*—bulb fennel—from our winter garden, and in the summer there are fine little radishes, so delicious to eat with good bread and butter. Another good vegetable, and one very classic for *crudités,* is celery root, grated and in a nice mayonnaise. For this rather rustic first course, the food processor is most useful, for grating the raw vegetable as well as for preparing the *nouvelle sauce verte.*

The gratinéed pork chops are a variation of a favorite dish of mine, which before the war I often enjoyed at a well-known, very Parisian restaurant called Chez Foyot. It was near the government Senate Chambers and also the Théatre de l'Odéon, and the most interesting crowd could often be found at lunch, a mixture of politicians and actors. The dish was originally made with veal chops, but since I know that in the United States it is easier to find pork of good quality than veal, I have adapted the dish for pork, though you can make it with veal if you choose. It demands little preparation, and can be assembled ahead to be gratinéed at the last moment. In place of the Swiss chard accompanying the dish, you could serve some nice buttered spinach.

The tart flavor of lemon at the end of a meal is quite refreshing, and very good for the digestion. The light *petites crèmes* are ready for the oven in a matter of minutes, and can be served right in their ramequins.

Le céleri-rave rémoulade

GRATED CELERY ROOT WITH
HERB MAYONNAISE

For 6:

1 pound (450 g) celery root
1 recipe *nouvelle sauce verte,*
   page 217

1 hard-boiled egg, peeled and
   pressed through a fine sieve
   into *mimosa* (optional)

Recommended equipment: A food processor equipped with the coarse grating blade (or a hand grater)

Peel the celery root deeply with a small, sharp knife, removing all of the tough skin. Slice into eighths and grate either in the food processor or by hand. Place in a bowl and toss with the prepared sauce. Chill for several hours to blend the flavors, although the celery root can be eaten right away. When you are ready to serve, turn into a serving dish and sprinkle with the *mimosa*.

Côtes de porc à la Foyot

GRATINÉED PORK CHOPS WITH ONIONS

For 6:

4 tablespoons (60 g) butter
½ cup (1 dL) cooking oil
2 pounds (900 g) onions, peeled
　and sliced
6 loin pork chops, 6 ounces
　(170 g) each, and about ¾
　inch (2 cm) thick
Salt and freshly ground pepper
1 cup (¼ L) dry white wine
1 cup (¼ L) veal or beef stock

(made from a bouillon cube,
　if you wish)
8 cloves garlic, peeled and
　minced
⅓ cup (40 g) stale bread
　crumbs
2 eggs plus 1 extra egg white
⅔ cup (60 g) grated Gruyère
　or Parmesan cheese
Several sprigs of parsley

Recommended equipment: 1 or 2 oval gratin dishes (or any other flat
ovenproof dish) large enough to hold the chops in one slightly overlapping layer

Heat half each of the butter and oil in a large skillet. Add the onions
and stir them for a minute or two over medium heat. Cover the pan,
lower the heat, and cook for 30 to 40 minutes, stirring from time to
time, until the onions are very tender and sweet. Uncover the pan and
raise the heat during the last 5 minutes of cooking to evaporate any
excess moisture.

　While the onions are cooking, prepare the chops. Trim away any
extra fat, then, using a small knife, score the edges of the meat to
prevent them from curling during the cooking. Pat the chops dry
with paper towels. In another skillet heat 3 tablespoons of oil over
medium-high heat and sauté the pork chops, three at a time, for 2
minutes on each side. The meat should just begin to feel firm to the

finger; do not overcook the chops now or they will be dry. When ready, remove to a flat pan or platter and season on both sides. Pour off the fat from the pan and deglaze with the wine.

When the onions are done add the deglazed juices from the pork to them, along with the stock and minced garlic, and continue cooking about 4 or 5 minutes, until the liquid has reduced by about one-half. Season the finished onions carefully and pour them into the gratin dish(es).

Press the bread crumbs firmly onto one side of each chop, then arrange the meat over the onions in one slightly overlapping layer, crumb side up. Pour over any juices accumulated around the chops. The dish may now wait for an hour or so at room temperature before finishing.

To gratiné the chops, beat the eggs with the extra white and remaining tablespoon of oil and season lightly with salt and pepper. Pour the beaten egg over the chops, sprinkle on the cheese, dot with the remaining butter, and bake in a 325°F (165°C) oven for 20 minutes, to finish cooking the chops and brown the cheese lightly. Run the dish under a hot broiler to give a nice crusty finish. Garnish with the sprigs of parsley and serve directly from the gratin dish.

Petites crèmes au citron

LEMON CREAMS IN RAMEQUINS

For 6:

Finely grated zest of 2 lemons
⅓ cup (¾ dL) lemon juice
3 eggs, separated, plus 2 extra
    yolks

2 tablespoons (30 g) unsalted
    butter
⅔ cup (125 g) granulated sugar
Pinch of salt
Powdered sugar (optional)

Recommended equipment: Six ½-cup (1 dL) porcelain ramequins (or Pyrex custard cups)

Butter the ramequins well. Put the grated zest, lemon juice, 5 egg yolks, butter, and ⅓ cup (65 g) of the sugar in a small, heavy-bottomed saucepan. Whisk over low heat until the mixture is hot to the fingers and thickens slightly; it should not boil. Remove the pan from the heat and whisk for a moment or two to cool the mixture and keep it from scrambling on the bottom.

Beat the egg whites with a pinch of salt until they form soft peaks. Sprinkle on the remaining sugar and continue beating until the whites form fairly stiff and shiny peaks. Delicately fold in the warm lemon mixture. Pour into the ramequins and bake in a 250°F (120°C) oven for 25 minutes, until just set. *It is essential that the ramequins cook in a very slow oven.* Serve warm or cold in the molds, sprinkled with a little powdered sugar.

Un dîner "les coudes sur la table"

A RELAXED DINNER FOR 6

✕

Fondue de champignons en enveloppe
CREAMY MUSHROOM TURNOVER

Palette de veau au paprika
VEAL FRICASSEE WITH PAPRIKA

Purée de céleri-rave
PURÉE OF CELERY ROOT

Timbale de riz "nouveau monde"
MOLDED RICE PUDDING WITH MAPLE
SYRUP AND MACADAMIA NUTS

Beaujolais "Juliénas"/Clos du Val Zinfandel

Un dîner *"les coudes sur la table"*

A RELAXED DINNER FOR 6

To have a meal *les coudes sur la table* means in France an occasion for close friends to linger over their food, chatting comfortably, with plenty of time to enjoy each dish. And this menu of hearty dishes is just the sort for such a warm and informal gathering.

The first course is a fairly substantial dish made with creamy mushrooms and a little soft scrambled egg wrapped up in pastry, which can be refrigerated overnight before baking. The fricassee of veal is gently flavored with paprika, and is served in a sauce of the reduced cooking liquid finished with sour cream. This kind of stew is ideal for entertaining because it can only gain in flavor by being made in advance and reheated. To accompany the veal is one of the best purées I know, a very delicate purée of celery root, with a little potato to give it body. It is useful to have this kind of dish in your repertoire, since, as the reheating demands no attention at all, it is the easiest way to do a vegetable in advance. A green salad is really all you need to follow the main course; if you would like a green vegetable with the veal, the *concombres au beurre* on page 43 would go very well.

The *timbale de riz "nouveau monde"* is simply a French rice pudding, which, in the classic version of my Normandy childhood, contained honey and almonds. The recipe is certainly very good done this way, but you will note that I have chosen to adapt it to two American ingredients I find irresistible: maple syrup and macadamia nuts. Once baked and unmolded, the pudding is given a light glaze with red-currant jelly; a little beaten *Chantilly* accompanies the dessert as well.

Fondue de champignons en enveloppe
CREAMY MUSHROOM TURNOVER

For 6:

1 recipe *pâte à croustade,*
  page 211
Double recipe creamy minced
  mushrooms, page 219
2 eggs

1½ teaspoons chopped fresh
  chives or ¼ teaspoon dried
  tarragon
⅛ teaspoon salt
Freshly ground pepper
Butter, if necessary

Recommended equipment: A small non-stick skillet; a baking sheet

Make the pastry. Measure out 12 ounces (340 g), wrap in plastic wrap, and refrigerate (store the remaining pastry for another use). Prepare the mushrooms as directed.

While the mushrooms are cooking, beat 1 egg lightly with your choice of herbs, the salt, and a bit of pepper. Pour into a small nonstick skillet (if you use a conventional skillet, add a little butter to the pan). Scramble the egg gently, stirring constantly until it has set softly. Set aside to cool.

Roll out a little more than one-half of the pastry about ⅛ inch (⅓ cm) thick, and trim it into an approximately 10-inch (25 cm) square. Set the pastry on a baking sheet and refrigerate to firm up while you roll out the other piece of dough to a slightly smaller square.

Remove the chilled pastry from the refrigerator and spread the scrambled egg over the center in a thin layer. Then spoon on the creamy mushrooms and spread them over the surface of the dough, leaving about a 1-inch (2½ cm) border all around. Lay the smaller square of pastry over this. Seal the edges by turning in the extended border of dough and pinching the pastry together. The prepared turnover may now wait for several hours or overnight in the re-

147

frigerator before being baked; it can go directly from the refrigerator to the oven.

To finish the *enveloppe,* beat the remaining egg with a fork and brush lightly over the dough; after a moment or two, paint on a second layer of the glaze. Score the surface of the pastry lightly with a small knife in a pretty pattern. If you wish, trim any leftover scraps of pastry into leaf shapes, press them onto the dough and also glaze. Bake in a 400°F (205°C) oven for 20 minutes (25 minutes if the turnover has been chilled), or until the turnover is a nice golden brown and the pastry is done. Allow to cool for a few minutes on a rack before serving. It can also be baked several hours in advance and served at room temperature.

Palette de veau au paprika

VEAL FRICASSEE WITH PAPRIKA

For 6 to 8:

3 pounds (1350 g) veal stew
   meat, cut into 2-inch (5 cm)
   pieces
3 cloves garlic, peeled
3 tablespoons Hungarian
   paprika
¼ cup (½ dL) peanut oil, more
   if necessary
1½ teaspoons salt
Freshly ground pepper
1 pound (450 g) onions, peeled
   and sliced

¼ cup (½ dL) bourbon or
   Cognac
1½ cups (3½ dL) dry white
   wine
2 cups (½ L) chicken or beef
   broth
Bouquet garni—parsley, fresh or
   dried thyme, bay leaf
⅓ cup (¾ dL) sour cream
1 tablespoon finely chopped
   fresh parsley

Recommended equipment: A 6- to 8-quart (6 to 8 L) ovenproof casserole with a lid

Trim the meat of any fat and gristle. Cut the garlic into slivers. Using a small, pointed knife, make an incision in each piece of meat and insert a piece of garlic. Pat the meat dry with paper towels, and turn each piece in the paprika to coat it evenly.

Heat the oil in the casserole over medium-high heat. Sear the pieces of veal in a single layer without crowding; if necessary, do this in two or three lots. As they are lightly browned on all sides, remove the pieces of meat from the pan, and season with the salt and pepper. Lower the heat slightly and if needed add an extra tablespoon or two of oil to the pan. Add the onions and cook them for 8 to 10 minutes, stirring occasionally, until they are lightly browned. Return the meat to the pan, pour on the bourbon or Cognac, and set it alight, shaking gently over heat until all of the alcohol has flamed away. Pour on the white wine and bring it to a simmer. Add the broth and *bouquet garni*. Place a piece of waxed paper or baking parchment directly on the surface of the meat, cover, then set the casserole in a 375°F (190°C) oven. Cook for 1 hour and 15 minutes to 1½ hours, until the meat is tender, turning the pieces once halfway through the cooking.

Discard the *bouquet garni*, then, using a slotted spoon or·skimmer, remove the meat and onions to a serving dish; cover lightly and keep warm. Degrease the cooking liquid, if necessary, and boil it down rapidly to about 1 cup (¼ L). Off heat swirl in the sour cream and correct the seasoning. Pour several spoonfuls of the sauce over the meat and onions, sprinkle with the parsley, and serve. Pass the remaining sauce in a sauceboat.

If you wish to cook the dish several hours before, or even the day ahead, when the meat is nearly done, remove the casserole to room temperature to cool. Then store, still covered, in the refrigerator. Remove to room temperature at least 1 hour before finishing the dish. To rewarm, return the cooking liquid to a simmer on top of the stove, then set the casserole in a 375°F (190°C) oven for 10 to 15 minutes. Finish the sauce and serve as directed.

Purée de céleri-rave

PURÉE OF CELERY ROOT

For 6:

1½ pounds (675 g) celery root
½ pound (225 g) boiling
   potatoes, peeled
⅔ cup (1½ dL) heavy cream

8 tablespoons butter (115 g) at
   room temperature
1¼ teaspoons salt
Freshly ground pepper

Recommended equipment: A food processor equipped with the metal blade (or a food mill)

Peel the celery root deeply with a small sharp knife, removing all of the tough skin. Cut both the root and the potatoes into rough 1-inch (2½ cm) pieces and cook in boiling salted water, partially covered, for about 15 minutes, until very tender when pierced with a knife. Drain thoroughly.

Purée the vegetables (still hot) in the food processor or put through the fine disk of a food mill. Add the cream, butter, and seasonings and whip to a fine purée. Correct the seasoning. If you wish to wait up to an hour or two before serving, press a piece of plastic wrap directly onto the surface of the purée. To reheat, place in a pan over medium heat and stir until hot.

Timbale de riz "nouveau monde"

MOLDED RICE PUDDING WITH MAPLE SYRUP
AND MACADAMIA NUTS

For 6 to 8:

⅓ cup (65 g) long-grain white
   rice
2 cups (½ L) heavy cream—or
   half milk and half cream
1 teaspoon cinnamon
⅔ cup (1½ dL) maple syrup
2 tablespoons (30 g) unsalted
   butter

3½ ounces (100 g) unsalted
   macadamia nuts (see page 14)
   or blanched almonds
4 eggs
¼ cup (½ dL) red-currant
   jelly
2 tablespoons orange liqueur
⅓ cup (¾ dL) heavy cream
2 tablespoons sugar
1 teaspoon vanilla

Recommended equipment: A 1-quart (1 L) metal charlotte mold (or any similar mold)

Line the bottom of the mold with a piece of buttered waxed paper or baking parchment, then smear the sides well with butter.

Add the rice to 1 quart (1 L) of boiling water and cook for 6 minutes, giving it an occasional stir. Drain the rice thoroughly in a colander. Bring the cream to a simmer in a medium-sized saucepan, along with the cinnamon, then stir in the rice and cook gently for 20 to 25 minutes, stirring frequently to prevent sticking on the bottom of the pan. The rice is done when it is very tender and creamy. Remove from the heat and stir in the maple syrup and the butter, cut into pieces.

While the rice is cooking, toast the macadamia nuts or almonds in a 350°F (175°C) oven until they are lightly brown. Allow the nuts to cool briefly, then pulverize in a food processor, or in small amounts in an electric blender, until they are quite fine. Beat in the eggs. Stir the nut mixture into the cooked rice, then pour into the prepared mold. Set the mold into a pan and pour simmering water around it to reach one-third up its sides. Bake in a 375°F (190°C) oven for 45 to 50 minutes, until the pudding is just set. The dessert will really be better if the center is slightly undercooked. Cool on a rack for at least 30 minutes before unmolding.

While the dessert cools, melt the red-currant jelly with the liqueur, stirring occasionally over low heat until smooth. Set aside to cool. When you are ready to serve, run a flexible metal spatula around the sides of the dessert and invert it onto a serving dish. Peel off the paper and paint the top and sides of the pudding with the glaze. Whip the cream with the sugar and vanilla until stiff. Slice the pudding into wedges, and serve with the *Chantilly*.

Un menu d'hiver autour du feu
A WINTER LUNCH BY THE HEARTH FOR 6

Saucisson de foies de volaille en brioche
CHICKEN- OR DUCK-LIVER ''SAUSAGE''
IN BRIOCHE

Hamburgers à la provençale
HAMBURGERS WITH LEFTOVER MEAT,
PROVENÇAL STYLE

Les fausses frites de Bramafam
OVEN POTATOES WITH A LITTLE GARLIC
(PAGE 44)

Salade verte
GREEN SALAD

Les poires en sabayon
PEARS WITH WINE-FLAVORED SABAYON

vin rouge de Cahors/Mayacamas
Cabernet Sauvignon

Un menu d'hiver autour du feu

A WINTER LUNCH BY THE HEARTH FOR 6

On chilly days at our farm in Provence my husband Jean and I always enjoy our meals together by the sitting room fire, and even when we entertain three or four close friends we still like to set the table near the cozy hearth. This winter menu is the sort I would serve for a lunch on such an occasion, for the dishes are informal and suited to a small gathering, and are very nourishing, too, for cold-weather appetites.

The liver sausage in brioche dough is a rustic version of the much grander *foie gras en brioche* that is known especially at holiday time in France. This simpler *saucisson* is good made with either chicken or duck livers, and when molded in *jet brioche* there are no long or complicated steps. Be sure, however, that the liver mixture is well chilled when it goes into the dough, as it will be much easier to handle. The little hamburgers that follow have the Provençal touches of garlic and fragrant herbs and are an excellent way to use up left-over meat; the tomato sauce will help keep the meat moist. While the accompanying *fausses frites* are not the traditional "fries," they are a tasty potato dish actually much easier to do.

I always like to serve a fruit dessert at lunchtime, and poached pears with a wine custard are a light finish to this substantial menu. (In summer this dessert would be very nice done with peaches.) I would poach the fruit in the same robust wine served with the dishes—and this is very French, at a simple meal, to drink and cook with a single wine; it will taste different with each dish, and by dessert time you will have warmed to it and enjoyed it many ways.

Saucisson de foies de volaille en brioche

CHICKEN- OR DUCK-LIVER ''SAUSAGE'' IN BRIOCHE

For 6:

1 recipe *jet brioche,* page 213
¾ pound (340 g) chicken or
  duck livers
8 tablespoons (115 g) unsalted
  butter
1¼ teaspoons salt
Freshly ground pepper

2 teaspoons *herbes de Provence*
  (see page 220)
3 tablespoons Cognac
½ cup (60 g) stale bread crumbs
1 egg yolk beaten with ½
  teaspoon water

Recommended equipment: A 7- to 8-cup (1¾ to 2 L) loaf pan

Make the brioche dough as directed, and while it is rising you can prepare the chicken or duck livers.

Clean the livers, removing any stringy bits. Melt 2 tablespoons (30 g) of the butter in a medium-sized skillet, add the livers, and sauté gently over medium heat for about 2 minutes on each side. Season with the salt, pepper, and herbs, then pour on the Cognac and set alight, shaking briefly over heat to evaporate all of the alcohol. Remove the pan from the heat and stir in the bread crumbs, allowing the livers to cool briefly before making a purée of them, either in a food processor or through the fine disk of a food mill. Beat in the remaining butter and correct the seasonings.

Spoon the liver mixture onto a piece of waxed paper and use the paper to pat it into a nice sausage shape slightly shorter than the loaf pan. Wrap the paper around and place in the freezer for 20 to 30 minutes to firm up.

Butter the loaf pan lightly. Deflate the brioche dough thoroughly on a lightly floured surface and pat it into a rough rectangular shape about 8 x 10 inches (20 x 25 cm)—it is really not necessary to use a rolling pin for this. Center the chilled liver "sausage" on the dough, then fold the sides over to meet and pinch the seam and the ends to seal. Place the brioche package in the buttered loaf pan, seam side down. Cover with a towel and set in a warm place until the dough has risen to fill the pan. This will take about 1 hour.

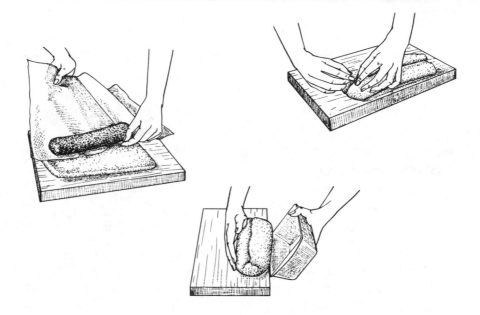

Brush the egg-yolk glaze onto the surface of the dough. Bake in a 400°F (205°C) oven for 40 minutes; the top should be nicely browned. Turn out onto a rack to cool for at least 1 hour before cutting it into slices with a serrated knife. The brioche loaf may wait several hours at room temperature before serving; you may rewarm it or not, as you like, and it is also very good eaten the next day.

Hamburgers à la provençale

HAMBURGERS WITH LEFTOVER MEAT,
PROVENÇAL STYLE

For 6:

1½ pounds (675 g) fresh
  spinach, stemmed and washed
2 tablespoons (30 g) butter
3 cloves garlic, peeled
Several sprigs of parsley
1½ pounds (675 g) cooked
  meat—beef, veal, or pork, or
  any combination
2 teaspoons *herbes de Provence*
  (see page 220)

3 eggs
Salt and freshly ground pepper
Pinch of cayenne
1 tablespoon paprika
½ cup (70 g) all-purpose flour
¼ cup (½ dL) peanut oil
1½ recipes quick tomato sauce,
  page 220

Recommended equipment: A large oval gratin dish (or other oven-proof dish)

Cook the spinach in boiling salted water for 3 to 4 minutes. Drain and refresh under cold running water, then drain again, thoroughly. Squeeze very dry in a strong kitchen towel and chop fairly fine either with a knife or in a food processor. Melt the butter in a skillet set over medium heat, then add the spinach, stirring to help evaporate the last of its moisture. Set aside.

Chop the garlic and parsley in the food processor, then the meat—in two lots if necessary. (Or if you are working by hand, chop the ingredients well with a knife.) Place the meat mixture in a mixing bowl, stir in the spinach, *herbes de Provence,* and eggs, then season highly with the salt, pepper, cayenne, and paprika. With your hands shape by 3 or 4 tablespoonfuls into little hamburgers; you should have about 20. Once made, the hamburgers may wait in the re-

157

frigerator for several hours or overnight. Remove them to room temperature at least 15 minutes before cooking them.

When you are ready to sauté the hamburgers, flour them lightly on each side (you will not use all of the flour). Heat the oil over medium-high heat in a large skillet and add as many hamburgers as the pan will hold without crowding them. Cook on each side for about 2 minutes. As they are done, remove to the gratin dish and continue with the others, layering them into the dish as they are cooked. The hamburgers may now wait for an hour or so at room temperature.

To finish, pour the tomato sauce over them and bake in a 375°F (190°C) oven for 12 to 15 minutes. Serve at once.

Les poires en sabayon

PEARS WITH WINE-FLAVORED SABAYON

For 6:

1½ cups (3½ dL) good red wine
1 cup (¼ L) water
A piece of orange rind studded with 2 cloves
⅓ cup (65 g) granulated sugar
3 ripe pears
2 teaspoons potato starch

3 egg yolks
3 to 4 tablespoons Poire William (pear brandy)
⅓ c (¾ dL) apricot jam, melted and cooled
3 tablespoons toasted sliced almonds

Recommended equipment: 6 individual dessert bowls

In a heavy-bottomed 3- to 4-quart (3–4 L) saucepan, bring the wine, water, orange rind, and sugar to a boil, then simmer for 10 minutes to make a light syrup. Peel and halve the pears and core them neatly. Poach in the syrup for 5 to 8 minutes, or just until tender. Transfer to a dish to drain while you reduce the syrup to 1½ cups (3½ dL).

In a small bowl, whisk the starch into the egg yolks, then beat them until they are slightly thick. Whisk in about half of the warm syrup, at first by drops and then in a steady stream. Return the mixture to the remaining syrup in the pan and whisk vigorously over moderate heat until the *sabayon* has thickened and is fluffy. Remove from the heat and stir in the brandy. Continue to beat for 3 or 4 minutes to cool the custard.

Divide the *sabayon* evenly among the bowls, and top with the pear halves. Brush each generously with the apricot glaze. Chill. Just before serving, sprinkle with the toasted almonds.

Un menu de dimanche en famille
A FAMILY SUNDAY DINNER FOR 8

X

Potage aux petits pois et aux fins légumes
FRESH PEA SOUP WITH AROMATIC
VEGETABLES

Nougat de boeuf
BEEF STEW WITH RED WINE
AND OLIVES

Nouilles au beurre
BUTTERED NOODLES

Pouding de tapioca aux poires, sauce à la groseille
TAPIOCA PUDDING WITH PEARS, KIRSCH,
AND RED-CURRANT SAUCE

Beaujolais/Joseph Phelps Zinfandel

Un menu de dimanche en famille

A FAMILY SUNDAY DINNER FOR 8

Family dinner on Sunday is something traditional in France, as I'm sure it is in the United States, and it is a time when children and parents can all be at home together and at the table. The weekend, too, is a lovely time for a *grasse matinée*—lazy morning—and so a Sunday menu with many of the dishes done the day before is always practical. Certainly a soup is an easy first course, and the *potage de petits pois aux fins légumes,* which can be made with either fresh or frozen peas, is the sort of warm start to a meal that I would serve in cooler months. In the summer, with beautiful tomatoes and radishes ready in the garden, I would not hesitate to substitute a pretty platter of raw vegetables for the soup. The *nougat de boeuf* is a tasty beef stew in red wine, with the olives at the end adding an interesting quality to the dish. The vegetables that cook with the meat are puréed to bind the sauce and enrich the flavor, which I feel gives a light and satisfactory result. The stew would be at its best if made the day before and reheated, to allow the meat to absorb all of the flavors. If you wish a vegetable accompaniment as well as the buttered noodles, fresh broccoli would go nicely with the beef.

The menu is completed with a soft tapioca dessert with pears, accompanied by a bright sauce made with red-currant jelly and a reduction of red wine. You needn't worry about two dishes with red wine in the same menu; the flavors are quite different. You could, of course, always choose to cook the fruit in a simple sugar syrup instead and make the sauce only with the red-currant jelly and kirsch.

Potage aux petits pois et aux fins légumes

FRESH PEA SOUP WITH AROMATIC VEGETABLES

For 6 to 8:

3 pounds (1350 g) fresh peas, in shells

2 quarts (2 L) chicken broth (made from bouillon cubes, if you wish)

¼ pound (115 g) bacon

1 medium-sized carrot, peeled

1 small onion, peeled

½ pound (225 g) leeks, trimmed and washed

1½ tablespoons cooking oil

Bouquet garni—parsley, fresh or dried thyme, bay leaf

2 tablespoons arrowroot

⅔ cup (1½ dL) milk or heavy cream

Salt and freshly ground pepper

Recommended equipment: A food processor equipped with the metal blade; or a food mill

Shell the peas; you should have about 3 cups. Bring the chicken broth to a boil in a large saucepan, add the peas, and cook them for 5 to 10 minutes, until they are quite tender; the cooking time will depend on the size and quality of the peas. Set a colander over a large bowl and drain (reserve the chicken stock for later). Purée the peas in a food processor or put through the medium disk of a food mill, using a few tablespoons of broth to smooth out the purée. Set aside.

Blanch the bacon for 3 or 4 minutes, covered with simmering water. Drain, pat dry, and cut into fine dice. Mince the carrot and onion in a food processor or by hand. Dice the leeks with a knife. Heat the oil in the saucepan and add the onion, carrots, leeks, and bacon. Cook over medium-low heat, partially covered with a lid, for 8 to 10 minutes, stirring occasionally. Add the chicken broth and *bouquet garni* and simmer for 10 to 15 minutes, until the vegetables are quite tender. Remove the *bouquet garni* from the pan.

In a small bowl, gradually stir the milk or cream into the arrowroot to dissolve it thoroughly. Add to the soup, along with the pea purée, and whisk over heat until it simmers and thickens slightly. Season with salt and pepper. (If the chicken broth was fairly salty, be careful not to oversalt at this point.)

The soup is good served as it is, with the slight texture of the *fins légumes*. If you prefer a more delicate soup, put through the fine disk of a food mill or purée in an electric blender. Serve hot.

Nougat de boeuf

BEEF STEW WITH RED WINE AND OLIVES

For 8:

⅓ cup (¾ dL) olive oil
½ pound (225 g) fresh salt pork, cut into *lardons* (small strips)
¼ pound (115 g) carrots, peeled and cut in thick slices
¾ pound (340 g) onions, peeled and quartered
2 cloves, stuck in a piece of onion
4 pounds (1800 g) beef stewing meat—chuck or bottom round —cut into 2-inch (5 cm) pieces
1 bottle good red wine— Beaujolais or Zinfandel

Bouquet garni—parsley, fresh or dried thyme, bay leaf
A piece of dried orange peel
1 tablespoon tomato paste
1 head of garlic (about 15 cloves)
10 to 12 peppercorns
2 cups (½ L) rich veal or beef broth
¾ cup (135 g) tiny *niçoise* olives or other good black olives, pitted
Salt and freshly ground pepper
Chopped fresh parsley

Recommended equipment: A 6- to 8-quart (6–8 L) flameproof casserole with a lid

Heat the olive oil in the casserole over medium heat. Add the *lardons* of salt pork and sauté them for 3 to 4 minutes, until they have rendered much of their fat and are beginning to brown. Toss in the carrots and onions and continue stirring over the heat for 5 or 6 minutes to brown. Using a skimmer or slotted spoon, transfer the vegetables and pieces of pork to a dish.

Pat the pieces of meat dry with paper towels and sear them in two or three lots on all sides in the hot oil, taking care not to crowd the pan. Remove the meat to a dish and season lightly. Pour off the fat from the casserole and add the bottle of wine, scraping the bottom of the pan with a wooden spoon to deglaze. Bring the wine to a simmer, then return the meat to the pan, along with the vegetables and salt pork, *bouquet garni,* orange peel, tomato paste, garlic, and peppercorns. Pour in the meat broth and any additional water needed to cover. Bring the liquid back to a simmer, place a piece of waxed paper or baking parchment over the meat, cover, and cook in a 350°F (180°C) oven for 1½ to 2 hours, until the meat is tender but not falling apart. Turn the pieces of meat once or twice as they cook.

When the meat is done, remove it to a serving dish to keep warm. Strain the liquid into a saucepan, reserving the vegetables and *lardons;* discard the *bouquet garni.* Remove the *lardons* and add them to the meat. Purée the vegetables through the fine disk of a food mill and then beat them until they are very smooth either in a food processor or an electric blender. Set aside.

Degrease the cooking liquid and boil it down to 2 cups (½ L). Whisk in the puréed vegetables and add the olives. Correct the seasoning. Pour the hot sauce over the meat, sprinkle with the parsley, and serve with buttered noodles.

The dish can be made ahead of time and stored for a day or two in the refrigerator. When you wish to reheat, allow it to come to room temperature, then bring to a simmer on top of the stove and heat in a moderate oven for 10 to 15 minutes. If the sauce is very thick, you may need to thin it slightly with a little water or broth.

Pouding de tapioca aux poires, sauce à la groseille

TAPIOCA PUDDING WITH PEARS, KIRSCH, AND
RED-CURRANT SAUCE

For 6 to 8:

2 cups (½ L) red wine
1 cup (200 g) granulated sugar
1 teaspoon cinnamon
2 ripe pears
1½ cups (3½ dL) milk
2 teaspoons vanilla extract
⅓ cup (70 g) quick-cooking
   tapioca

5 tablespoons (70 g) unsalted
   butter at room temperature
4 eggs, separated
Pinch of salt
½ cup (1 dL) imported kirsch
   or Poire William (pear
   brandy)
½ cup (1 dL) red-currant jelly

Recommended equipment: a 2-quart (2 L) porcelain soufflé dish (or other similar baking dish)

Butter the soufflé dish generously. Bring the wine, ½ cup (100 g) of the sugar, and the cinnamon to a simmer in a medium-sized saucepan. Peel and quarter the pears, remove the cores, then slice the quarters in half lengthwise. Add to the simmering wine and poach until tender when pierced with a small knife, about 5 to 8 minutes, depending on the quality of the pears. When they are done, remove with a skimmer to a tray or bowl to cool. Reduce the wine syrup over high heat to about ½ cup (1 dL); set aside.

    Put the milk, vanilla, and tapioca in another saucepan and allow to stand for 5 minutes. Then bring to a boil, stirring constantly, and continue cooking over medium-low heat until the mixture thickens, about 2 to 3 minutes Off heat stir in the butter, a tablespoon at a time, then the egg yolks, one at a time, and 5 tablespoons of the kirsch. Beat the egg whites with a pinch of salt until they form soft peaks. Sprinkle on the remaining ½ cup (100 g) sugar and continue beating until the meringue will stand in fairly stiff, creamy peaks. Fold in the warm tapioca and pour into the prepared mold. Stand the pears in the pudding, and bake in a 375°F (190°C) oven for 30 to 35 minutes, until it has puffed slightly and is nicely browned; the center should remain a little soft. Remove to a rack to cool for at least 30 minutes before serving.

Whisk the reduced wine syrup with the red-currant jelly over medium heat for a minute or two to blend thoroughly. Add the remaining 3 tablespoons of kirsch and pour into a bowl or sauceboat. The sauce should be served warm but not too hot. To serve, spoon the dessert onto plates with a bit of the sauce poured over. The pudding is best when it is warm or tepid but can also be eaten cold.

Un menu
pour honorer une grosse légume

A MENU HONORING
AN IMPORTANT GUEST, FOR 8

✶

Avocats farcis aux fruits de mer
AVOCADOS STUFFED WITH SEAFOOD

vin blanc de la Loire—
Pouilly Fumé / Robert Mondavi Fumé Blanc Reserve

Gigot anglo-normand à la crème moutardée
POACHED LEG OF LAMB WITH MUSTARD
CREAM SAUCE AND TARRAGON

Palets de pommes de terre
SAUTÉED POTATO PANCAKES WITH
EGG AND ONION

Brocolis au beurre ou Purée de haricots verts
BUTTERED BROCCOLI OR
PURÉE OF GREEN BEANS (PAGE 6)

Chocolate snobbish
LIGHT CHOCOLATE CAKE WITH PRUNES
AND WHIPPED CREAM

Bordeaux rouge—
St. Julien / Van LobenSels
Cabernet Sauvignon

Un menu pour honorer une grosse légume

A MENU HONORING AN IMPORTANT GUEST, FOR 8

When one is lucky enough in life to know someone in high places, it never hurts to have a very fancy menu in your repertoire—one where the dishes are quite refined or a bit unusual—to flatter a terribly important personage at your table. I myself have given a few dinners of this sort over the years, and I remember one especially when my husband was decorated by the Legion of Honor for distinction in military service during the war. After the ceremony I gave a dinner for Jean's colonel with the best dishes I could manage in those postwar years, which surely could not have included anything so rare as avocados. But I did serve this special leg of lamb (which I probably went all the way to Normandy for!), and the dessert would unquestionably have been chocolate, as in this present menu.

The first course—combining avocado with fruits of the sea and the refreshing flavor of lime—is a California classic I have made my own with a few touches of Provence—the good taste of fruity olive oil with some fresh basil. I would certainly serve these avocados in the American style, which I find so practical, with the prettily garnished plates already on the table when the guests sit down.

The Anglo-Saxon influences in my native province of Normandy are certainly evident in the lamb dish for this menu, for boiling meat is a very English way of cooking. I prefer the word "poach," however, to describe a leg of lamb cooked for only *12 minutes per pound* in a nicely flavored broth. In this fashion the meat is not gray but still pink and juicy. The Norman touch in this dish is the delicate cream sauce with tarragon, perhaps surprising with red meat. An impressive way to serve the lamb is to carve it and arrange the slices—neatly overlapping to show some of the nice pink meat—along the carved leg set on a beautiful platter garnished with one of the vegetables, the broccoli for instance, and sprigs of watercress.

The *chocolate snobbish* is a light cake with prunes stuffed with toasted almonds poked here and there into the batter. The garnish of *Chantilly* can be as fanciful or as simple as you like, although plenty of swirls will dress up the cake and make it live up to its name.

Avocats farcis aux fruits de mer

AVOCADOS STUFFED WITH SEAFOOD

For 8:

4 large, ripe avocados
Juice of 3 limes, more if
   necessary
¼ pound (115 g) fresh
   mushrooms, washed and with
   stems trimmed
½ pound (225 g) bay shrimp,
   prawns, or crayfish, cooked
   and shelled
½ pound (225 g) fresh or
   canned crab meat
¼ pound (115 g) pitted green
   olives

3 tablespoons chopped fresh
   herbs plus several whole
   sprigs—parsley with basil or
   chervil
½ cup (115 g) chopped walnuts
   plus 8 halves; or sliced or
   slivered toasted almonds
¾ cup (150 g) long-grain white
   rice
¼ cup (½ dL) olive oil
2 to 2½ teaspoons salt
Freshly ground pepper
A few drops of Tabasco

Slice the avocados in half, remove the seeds, and scoop out the flesh. Dice coarsely and sprinkle with a few drops of the lime juice. Reserve the avocado shells.

Slice the mushrooms thin and put them to marinate in the lime juice. If you are using prawns or crayfish tails, slice them in half lengthwise. Pick over the crabmeat, discarding any bits of shell and shredding the meat with your fingers. Slice the olives into fine slivers.

Reserve for garnishing a spoonful of the olives, a spoonful of the chopped herbs, the walnut halves or a few of the almonds, and a few of the shellfish or crayfish tails.

Bring 2 quarts (2 L) of water with a tablespoon of salt to a boil and stir in the rice. Boil for 15 to 18 minutes, or until just tender. Drain and rinse briefly under cold running water. Drain again thoroughly.

In a large bowl, combine the avocado, raw mushrooms in their marinade, shellfish or crayfish tails, olives, rice, olive oil, and herbs and seasonings, along with the nuts. Stir the mixture together well and correct the seasoning, adding extra lime juice as needed. Heap the mixture into the avocado shells, smoothing it into a generous mound. Once filled, the avocados may wait for an hour or two in the refrigerator before serving. If you wish to prepare the dish a day in advance, it would be best to store the filling in a covered bowl, and then fill the avocado shells just before serving.

Decorate the dish with the reserved garnish and sprigs of herbs, and serve slightly chilled (but not too cold).

Variation: Ananas farci (Stuffed pineapple). This is also an attractive dish presented in scooped-out pineapple halves, with the leaves still attached, set on a platter decorated with watercress. Use the fruit, diced or in balls, in place of the avocado. Heap the stuffing into mounds in the pineapple shells. Spoon onto plates.

Gigot anglo-normand à la crème moutardée

POACHED LEG OF LAMB WITH MUSTARD CREAM
SAUCE AND TARRAGON

For 8:

3 medium-sized carrots, well
  scrubbed
1 pound (450 g) turnips, peeled
2 medium-sized onions, peeled
2 stalks celery
Bouquet garni—parsley, fresh
  or dried thyme, bay leaf
1 tablespoon salt
1 teaspoon whole peppercorns

1 leg of lamb, 6 pounds (2¾ kg),
  trimmed of most fat
2½ cups (6 dL) heavy cream,
  more as necessary
2 or 3 small sprigs of fresh
  tarragon or 1 teaspoon dried
2 tablespoons tarragon mustard
Freshly ground pepper
½ teaspoon potato starch
  (optional)

Recommended equipment: An 8- to 10-quart (8–10 L) pot

Slice the vegetables roughly, place in the pot with the *bouquet garni,*
and add 4 to 5 quarts (4–5 L) water. Simmer for about 1 hour. After
half an hour, add the salt and peppercorns. Set aside until you are
ready to cook the lamb.

About 1½ hours before serving, bring the broth back to a boil and
add the leg of lamb. Simmer uncovered for 1 hour and 10 minutes for
rare lamb; the juice should still run pink. Remove from the pot and
keep covered in a warm place; the lamb should rest for 20 to 30 minutes before carving.

As the meat is cooking, begin the sauce: add the cream to a heavy-
bottomed 3-quart (3 L) saucepan and simmer over medium heat with
the tarragon. (If you are using fresh tarragon, reserve a few of the
leaves.) When reduced by about one-third and thickened slightly,
whisk in the mustard diluted with a tablespoon or two of additional

cream. If the poaching liquid seems especially good, whisk a few tablespoons of this into the sauce as well, to give it some extra flavor. Taste the sauce carefully for seasoning, adding fresh pepper, and salt if necessary. Thicken with the potato starch if needed. The sauce can wait for up to an hour at room temperature before serving.

When you are ready to serve, rewarm the sauce and remove the tarragon, if fresh sprigs have been used. Chop the reserved leaves of fresh tarragon and stir into the sauce. Carve the lamb and arrange it on a hot platter or as suggested in the introductory notes. Pass the sauce separately.

Palets de pommes de terre

SAUTÉED POTATO PANCAKES
WITH EGG AND ONION

For 8:

2 pounds (900 g) boiling
   potatoes, peeled
1 small onion, peeled
2 eggs
1½ teaspoons salt

Freshly ground pepper
1 tablespoon chopped fresh
   parsley
5 tablespoons peanut oil

Recommended equipment: A food processor with a grater; a large skillet

Finely grate the potatoes and then the onion, either in a food processor or by hand. Squeeze the vegetables dry in a strong kitchen towel and mix them in a bowl with the eggs, seasonings, and parsley. Heat the oil in a large skillet set over medium-high heat. Add the potato mixture to the pan by tablespoonfuls, flattening each into a neat oval shape with the back of a spoon or a metal spatula, and taking care not to crowd the skillet. Sauté the *palets* for 2 to 3 minutes on each side, until they are crisp and nicely brown. As they are done, remove them to absorbent paper to drain, and then keep warm on a platter. The sooner they are eaten the better they will be. If you wish to do them an hour ahead of time, you will want to crisp them up at the last minute over high heat, with some additional oil.

Chocolate snobbish

LIGHT CHOCOLATE CAKE WITH PRUNES AND WHIPPED CREAM

For a 9-inch (23 cm) cake serving 8:

10 blanched almonds, split
10 moist-pack pitted prunes
6 tablespoons imported kirsch
  or *mirabelle*
7 ounces (200 g) semisweet
  chocolate, broken into bits
2 tablespoons instant coffee
  granules
3 tablespoons water

4 eggs, separated
10 tablespoons (140 g) unsalted
  butter, at room temperature
Pinch of salt
½ cup (100 g) granulated sugar
½ cup (60 g) potato starch
⅔ cup (1½ dL) heavy cream
2 tablespoons powdered sugar
¼ teaspoon vanilla extract

Recommended equipment: A 9-inch (23 cm) cake pan

Line the bottom of the pan with a piece of buttered waxed paper, then butter the sides thoroughly.

Place the almonds in a shallow pan and toast them in a 375°F (190°C) oven for 6 to 8 minutes, until they are a rich golden brown. Meanwhile, place the prunes and the kirsch or *mirabelle* in a small saucepan, bring to a simmer, then remove from the heat. Ignite the alcohol and allow to flame gently for a few moments, then clamp a lid on the pan. Set aside to cool.

When the almonds are ready, allow them to cool briefly. Remove the prunes from the brandy (reserve the liquid), pat dry, then cut each in half and roll around one of the almond halves. Set aside.

In a heavy-bottomed saucepan, melt the chocolate with the instant coffee and water over low heat, stirring frequently. Off heat add the egg yolks, one at a time, then return the pan to the heat and stir the mixture for a minute or two to warm the yolks and thicken the chocolate. Remove the pan from the heat and stir in the butter, a tablespoon at a time. Add the reserved prune liquor.

Beat the egg whites with a pinch of salt until they form soft peaks. Sprinkle on the granulated sugar and continue beating the whites until they form stiff peaks. Beat in the starch. Fold the warm chocolate into the beaten whites, then turn the batter into the prepared pan. Poke the stuffed bits of prune into the batter in 2 neat circles.

Bake in a 375°F (190°C) oven for 25 to 30 minutes; the cake will have puffed nicely and should remain slightly creamy in the center. Don't overcook. Remove to a rack to cool for a good hour (the surface will crack slightly as it settles back into the pan), then unmold onto a platter and remove the paper. Whip the cream with the powdered sugar and vanilla and spread half of it into a neat layer on top of the cake; pipe on the remaining *Chantilly* in pretty swirls, using a pastry bag. Keep the dessert refrigerated until 30 minutes before serving.

Like most chocolate cakes, the *snobbish* will be even better if made the day before.

Un buffet de fête en plein air

A GALA OPEN-AIR BUFFET FOR 10 TO 12

Les billes de macadamia
MACADAMIA NUT AND BLUE CHEESE BALLS

La pizza Jeannette
PIZZA WITH ONIONS, TOMATOES, CHEESE,
AND NIÇOISE OLIVES (PAGE 33)

Pâté de porc aux blettes et à la crème
PORK PÂTÉ WITH SWISS CHARD AND CREAM

Épaule de veau farcie et roulée
BRAISED VEAL SHOULDER STUFFED WITH
ZUCCHINI AND MUSHROOMS

Gratin de brocolis
BAKED PURÉE OF BROCCOLI AND POTATO

Haricots verts et tomates en salade
GREEN BEAN AND TOMATO SALAD

Biscuit glacé au sorbet rose
RASPERRY ICE WITH PEAR ICE CREAM
AND LADYFINGERS

tout au champagne—un grand blanc de blancs/
Beaulieu Champagne de Chardonnay

Un buffet de fête en plein air

A GALA OPEN-AIR BUFFET FOR 10 TO 12

I love to entertain in the summertime, when I can offer my guests a glass of champagne on the lawn and serve them colorful dishes on a buffet table set under the olive trees. On such occasions it seems essential to plan dishes that can be completed easily one or two days in advance, so that the atmosphere is at its most relaxed for the host or hostess and the guests. All of the dishes in this buffet menu, then, I have chosen especially because they can be done with the help of the food processor and made ahead of time: the macadamia balls, the veal (if it is served cold), the broccoli and the frozen dessert, one day before; the pâté, at least two days, and preferably three days, for the fullest flavor.

Along with the *pizza Jeannette,* cut into little squares, the *billes de macadamia* are a pleasant little cocktail bite to serve with *apéritifs:* and certainly instead of an imported blue cheese you could use one of the good domestic ones—perhaps from Oregon, and I understand there is also a nice blue cheese from Wisconsin. The pork pâté, with the green of the chard and the texture of the livers, is an appealing dish for a buffet when it is unmolded and sliced; it contains a little cream, which gives lightness and a more delicate flavor. As for the veal shoulder, it can be stuffed and rolled the day before without any problem, as it contains a mostly vegetable stuffing. Then, it is a simple matter to braise it two hours before serving and keep it warm until slicing. Certainly, too, the veal is delicious cold, in which case it could be completely cooked the day before and will be very easy to serve, prettily garnished on a platter; directions for this are given at the end of the recipe. To accompany the veal there is a nice green gratin of puréed broccoli, with a little potato to give it texture. I must say I am very fond of this American vegetable, and while the stems and florets are good served whole, I feel it is a pleasant change and the broccoli somehow more refined when puréed. It should, in any case, always be carefully peeled, to shorten the cooking time and help it keep its color. The vegetable salad will be welcome after the veal in its sauce, and for this I am fortunate to have from my own garden wonderfully sweet tomatoes, and the tiniest little green beans by the bushel all summer long. If you have difficulty finding good tomatoes and beans, I would encourage you to use any fine summer vegetables suitable for a salad that you can find. I recommend the *nouvelle sauce verte* on page 217 for the dressing, which you may want to thin down with a little extra vinegar or lemon juice for this type of salad (if you are serving the veal cold, however, with the herb-mustard sauce as suggested, then you would of course use a simple vinaigrette for the vegetables).

The raspberry and pear *biscuit glacé* I first made in one of my cooking classes in the Napa Valley one warm autumn evening when we felt a special longing for something cool. It is not at all difficult to accomplish, but for the ladyfingers you should have good homemade ones, a recipe for which is given. The base for the dessert is an Italian meringue, half of which becomes an ice cream with pears, while the other half receives an intensely flavored purée of raspberry.

Les billes de macadamia

MACADAMIA AND BLUE-CHEESE BALLS

For about 40 billes:

3 ounces (85 g) macadamia nuts
2½ to 3 ounces (70–85 g) blue
  cheese
8 tablespoons (115 g) unsalted
  butter
A few drops of Tabasco
Freshly ground pepper

¼ teaspoon paprika
3 Ry-Krisp crackers
Several sprigs of parsley
A small amount of chives (to
  make about 1 tablespoon,
  chopped)

Recommended equipment: A food processor equipped with the metal blade

Place the macadamia nuts in a single layer on a baking sheet and toast them in a 350°F (180°C) oven for 8 to 10 minutes, shaking them occasionally, until they are a light golden brown. Remove to room temperature, allow to cool, then chop fine—for about 5 seconds, or so, in the food processor—or by hand. Add the blue cheese and the butter, cut into pieces, and blend the mixture well. Season (salt may not be necessary) and turn the mixture into a mixing bowl. Set in the refrigerator to chill.

Chop the Ry-Krisp in the food processor, along with the fresh herbs, until fine. Shape the macadamia-cheese mixture into balls (a melon baller would be useful for this) and then roll them in the Ry-Krisp and herb mixture. Refrigerate until 5 to 10 minutes before you are ready to serve; they should not be too firm. Place a toothpick in each *bille.*

Pâté de porc aux blettes et à la crème

PORK PÂTÉ WITH SWISS CHARD AND CREAM

For 12 to 14:

2 pounds (900 g) Swiss chard greens, thoroughly washed
¼ pound (115 g) chicken livers
¼ cup (½ dL) bourbon or Cognac
Salt and freshly ground pepper
1 pound (450 g) fresh pork, half fat and half lean
½ pound (225 g) good boiled ham
¼ pound (115 g) bacon
2 cloves garlic, peeled and finely chopped
1 tablespoon *herbes de Provence* (see page 220)

1 tablespoon chopped fresh tarragon or 1 teaspoon dried
4 eggs
1 cup (¼ L) heavy cream
Pinch of cayenne
Freshly grated nutmeg
5 tablespoons port
3 thin strips of pork fat, each approximately 6 x 8 inches (15 x 20 cm)
¼ pound (115 g) prosciutto in one piece, cut into long strips
1 bay leaf
1 cup (140 g) flour

Recommended equipment: A food processor or meat grinder; an 8-cup (2 L) oval or rectangular terrine with a lid (porcelain or glass); an electric mixer with a flat beating attachment

Plunge the Swiss chard into 3 or 4 quarts (3 to 4 L) of boiling salted water and cook for 4 to 5 minutes, or until tender. Drain, refresh briefly under cold running water, and drain again, thoroughly. Then give the greens a good squeeze—a handful at a time—in a strong kitchen towel to remove most of the water. Chop roughly, in a food processor or by hand. Set aside.

Pick through the chicken livers, removing any stringy bits, then marinate in the bourbon or Cognac with a few generous grinds of pepper.

Slice the fresh pork into 2-ounce (60 g) pieces, and grind it in the food processor—in two batches—or in a meat grinder until it is nicely chopped; it should retain a little texture and not be a purée. Remove the pork to a large mixing bowl, then coarsely grind the boiled ham and bacon and add to the bowl. Using your hands, a hefty wooden spatula, or, if you have it, a mixer with a flat beater, blend the meat mixture together with the chard, garlic, herbs, the eggs (beaten lightly with the cream), 1 to 1½ teaspoons salt, pepper to taste, the cayenne, nutmeg, port, and the marinating liquid. Sauté a spoonful for tasting, if you wish; the pork must, of course, be cooked.

Line the sides and bottom of a terrine with the pork fat. (If you have difficulty finding pork fat, a good substitute is a double thickness of cheesecloth dipped in melted lard or vegetable shortening and set in the freezer to solidify.) Pack in one-third of the pâté mixture, then arrange down the center half of the chicken livers and half of the prosciutto strips. Make another layer with another third of the pâté mixture, add the remaining livers and strips of prosciutto, and top with the last of the pâté mixture. Give the terrine several solid taps against the working surface to help settle the contents, top with the bay leaf, and cover.

Stir 5 tablespoons water into the flour to make a very rough, sticky dough. Pat the flour paste all around the lid of the terrine to seal it tightly, then place the dish in a pan and pour boiling water around it to reach about halfway up the sides. Bake in a 375°F (190°C) oven for 1½ hours. When the pâté is pricked, the juices should run clear and not rosy.

Remove the terrine to a rack, break away the flour seal, and place a good weight on the pâté to pack it down as it cools. When it is cold, place it in the refrigerator, where it will keep very well for at least 2 weeks.

Before serving the pâté, it is really best to wait 2 or 3 days, when the flavors will be richer and the texture more settled. Serve directly from the terrine or unmolded onto a platter.

Épaule de veau farcie et roulée

BRAISED VEAL SHOULDER STUFFED WITH
ZUCCHINI AND MUSHROOMS

For 10:

For the veal and stuffing:

4 pounds (1800 g) boned
   shoulder of veal, trimmed of
   all fat and gristle
2½ tablespoons Dijon mustard
¾ pound (340 g) zucchini,
   trimmed and washed
Salt
2 tablespoons finely minced
   shallots
2 tablespoons (30 g) butter
1 tablespoon cooking oil
1 recipe creamy minced
   mushrooms, page 219
1 ounce (30 g) fresh white

bread, trimmed of the crusts
   and coarsely grated
2 tablespoons heavy cream
¼ pound (115 g) boiled ham,
   diced
½ cup (45 g) grated Parmesan
   cheese
1 egg
1 tablespoon chopped fresh
   parsley
1 tablespoon chopped fresh
   chives or dill
Freshly ground pepper
Freshly grated nutmeg

For braising:

5 tablespoons cooking oil
2 carrots, scrubbed and cut into
   quarters
2 medium-sized onions, peeled
   and sliced
Bouquet garni—parsley, fresh or
   dried thyme, bay leaf

1½ cups (3½ dL) dry white
   wine
2 cups (½ L) good veal or
   chicken stock
5 tablespoons (70 g) butter
Sprigs of watercress

Recommended equipment: A roasting pan or casserole with a lid, large enough to hold a 14-inch (35 cm) roast

Lay the veal shoulder flat on a working surface and slice partially through the thickest section of meat to increase the surface for stuffing. Coat the surfaces of the meat with the mustard; set in the refrigerator while you prepare the stuffing.

Grate the zucchini in a food processor or by hand, then toss it in a colander with 1 teaspoon salt. Allow to drain for 10 minutes, then squeeze very dry in a strong kitchen towel. In a skillet, sauté the shallots gently in the butter and oil for about 2 minutes, then stir in the zucchini and cook for 6 to 8 minutes, until just tender. Correct the seasoning, being careful not to oversalt.

Prepare the mushrooms as directed. In a mixing bowl, combine the cooked zucchini, mushrooms, bread, cream, ham, Parmesan cheese, egg, and herbs. Taste the stuffing carefully for seasoning, adding salt, pepper, and nutmeg as needed. Spread the mixture evenly over the surface of the meat, then roll it up in a large piece of cheesecloth and tie it firmly with string at intervals along its length to make a plump sausage shape about 14 inches (35 cm) long.

Heat the 5 tablespoons oil in the pan and brown the meat on all sides. Remove from the pan and add the carrots and onions, stirring over medium heat to brown them lightly, for 8 to 10 minutes. Return the meat to the pan. It can wait for up to an hour or two before it is braised. When you are ready to continue, add the *bouquet garni* to the pan along with the wine and bring to a boil, scraping the bottom of the pan to deglaze it. Pour in the stock and return to a boil. Lay a piece of waxed paper directly over the meat, cover with a lid, and cook in a 375°F (190°C) oven for 1¼ to 1½ hours. The liquid should maintain a slow simmer; turn the veal once midway during its cooking.

When the meat is done, set it in a warm place, covered with foil, to rest; it may wait up to 45 minutes. Strain the vegetables from the braising liquid (the onions may be served with the meat, if you wish). If necessary, degrease the liquid, then boil it down rapidly to about 1⅓ cups (3¼ dL). Off heat swirl in the butter; correct the seasoning. Remove the strings and cheesecloth from the veal, carve it into neat slices, and arrange them on a hot platter. Mask with a bit of the sauce and garnish with the watercress. Pass the remaining sauce in a sauceboat.

To serve the veal cold, boil the braising liquid down to about ½ cup (1 dL), until it is a glaze. Omit the butter enrichment, and when the concentrated liquid has cooled and is beginning to set, brush it on the cold slices of veal arranged on a platter. Serve with the *nouvelle sauce verte* on page 217.

Gratin de brocolis

BAKED PURÉE OF BROCCOLI AND POTATO

For 10 to 12:

2 pounds (900 g) boiling potatoes, peeled	½ cup (1 dL) heavy cream
2½ to 3 pounds (1125–1350 g) fresh broccoli	2½ teaspoons salt
	Freshly ground pepper
6 tablespoons (85 g) soft butter	Freshly grated nutmeg
4 eggs	⅓ cup (30 g) grated Gruyère cheese

Recommended equipment: a food processor with the metal blade or a food mill; a large oval gratin dish

Slice the potatoes into rough 1-inch (2½ cm) square pieces and cook them in a large quantity of boiling salted water for 15 to 18 minutes, until very tender when pierced with a knife. Drain thoroughly (reserve the cooking water).

While the potatoes cook, use a small, sharp knife to trim the stems of broccoli and peel away the tough, stringy skin. Halve or quarter the stems, depending on their thickness; trim the heads of broccoli into neat florets. When the potatoes are done, boil all the broccoli in the reserved water for about 5 to 6 minutes, until it is very tender. Drain and plunge into cold water, then drain thoroughly and squeeze dry in the corner of a strong kitchen towel.

Purée the broccoli and potatoes either in a food processor (you may need to do this in two batches) or put through the medium disk of a food mill. Beat in 4 tablespoons (60 g) of the butter, then the eggs, cream, and seasonings. Butter the gratin dish and pour in the broccoli mixture, which may wait for an hour or two at room temperature. Or it may be covered with plastic wrap and refrigerated for several hours or overnight. Be sure to remove to room temperature at least 1 hour before finishing.

To bake the purée, sprinkle on the cheese, dot with the remaining butter, and set in a 400°F (205°C) oven for 15 to 20 minutes, then run under a hot broiler to brown lightly. Serve from the dish.

Biscuit glacé au sorbet rose

RASPBERRY ICE WITH PEAR ICE CREAM
AND LADYFINGERS

For 10 to 12:

3 pints (1½ L) fresh
   raspberries or 1½ pounds
   (750 g) frozen raspberries,
   thawed
2 ripe pears, peeled and cored
Juice of 1 lemon
1 cup (190 g) granulated sugar
4 egg whites
Pinch of salt

½ cup (1 dL) heavy cream
¼ c (30 g) powdered sugar
½ cup (1 dL) imported kirsch
   or Poire William (pear
   brandy)
24 to 30 ladyfingers, preferably
   homemade (see page 201)
Sprigs of fresh mint

Recommended equipment: Two 6-cup (1½ L) rectangular metal molds, about 12 inches (30 cm) long; an electric mixer

Line the bottom of the mold with waxed paper. If you are using fresh raspberries, *it is best not to wash them,* as this will only dilute their flavor. Set aside 12 or so whole raspberries to be used as a garnish. Purée the remaining berries in a food processor and then put through a fine sieve, or else put them through the fine disk of a food mill. You should have about 2½ cups (6 dL); reserve 1 cup (¼ L) of the purée for the sauce. Purée the pears in the processor or put through a food mill (medium disk), and stir in the lemon juice. Set the purées in the refrigerator to chill.

For the *meringue italienne,* bring the sugar and ⅓ cup (¾ dL) water to a boil in a small saucepan without stirring, and cook for about 2 minutes, until the syrup runs off a spoon in a slightly sticky stream. Meanwhile, beat the egg whites to soft peaks with a pinch of salt, preferably using an electric beater. Beating steadily, pour the boiling syrup in a continuous stream into the whites, and continue beating for 2 to 3 minutes, until the meringue has cooled and is stiff and shiny. If you wish, place the bowl in ice water to speed this along. Set the meringue in the refrigerator.

With the electric beater (you needn't wash it) whip the cream in a large bowl, sprinkling on the powdered sugar and adding ¼ cup (¾ dL) kirsch or Poire as it stiffens. Delicately fold the pear purée into the cream, then fold in half of the cold meringue. Fold the raspberry purée into the remaining meringue.

Sprinkle the underside of the ladyfingers with the remaining kirsch or Poire—whichever you have used. Line the bottom of one of the molds with some of the ladyfingers and spoon in half of the pear cream. Make another layer of ladyfingers and spoon in half of the raspberry mixture; finish with more ladyfingers. Repeat the layers for the second mold. Set in the freezer for at least 4 hours; the dessert should be firm enough to unmold, yet the texture will be better if not frozen too solid.

To serve, run a spatula around the edges of the molds, and invert onto a platter. Spoon some of the reserved raspberry purée—slightly sweetened, if you wish, and thinned with a little additional liquor —over and around the dessert. Dust the whole raspberries with powdered sugar and arrange them prettily, along with the fresh mint. Serve in slices. Pass any remaining purée.

An Encore of Desserts

※

Gâteau élégant au citron

Reine de macadamia

Le Montmorency

Le gâteau aux pommes "Jeanina"

Le gâteau des Acadiens

La tarte aux pommes de St. Tropez

Soufflé rocambole aux poires

Petits biscuits à l'orange

La Marquise enrubannée

Les petits fours

Gâteau élégant au citron

LEMON MACAROON CAKE

This is a dressy and yet rather easy cake to make, not too sweet, and with a slightly chewy quality, the base being a kind of macaroon mixture of meringue and pulverized almonds, with a rich lemon cream to finish it off.

For a 9-inch (23 cm) cake:

5 eggs, separated	Grated zest of 4 lemons
Pinch of salt	12 tablespoons (170 g) unsalted
1¾ cup (335 g) granulated	butter, cut into pieces
sugar	¼ cup (½ dL) lemon juice
½ cup (70 g) all-purpose flour	⅓ cup (¾ dL) dark rum
⅓ cup (40 g) potato starch	1 ounce (30 g) pistachios
3 ounces (85 g) almonds	

Recommended equipment: A 9-inch (23 cm) cake pan

Place a piece of buttered waxed paper or baking parchment on the bottom of the pan, then butter the sides well.

Beat the egg whites with the pinch of salt until they form soft peaks. Gradually sprinkle on 1 cup (190 g) of the sugar as you continue beating to form a firm and shiny meringue. Sift together the flour and starch; pulverize the almonds in a food processor or electric blender. Delicately fold the flour mixture and almonds, along with the grated zest of 3 lemons, into the meringue, stirring gently at the same time to mix all together well. Turn into the prepared pan and bake in a 350°F (180°C) oven for 15 minutes, then raise the heat to 400°F (205°C) and continue baking for another 20 minutes. The cake is done when a knife inserted in the center comes out clean. Allow to cool in the pan 15 minutes before turning out onto a rack.

While the cake is baking, prepare the lemon cream. Place the egg yolks, remaining sugar and lemon zest, butter, and lemon juice in a heavy-bottomed saucepan and whisk constantly over low heat until the mixture thickens slightly and is hot to the finger; it should not boil. Remove from the heat and whisk for a few moments to cool the mixture and keep it from scrambling on the bottom. Turn into a bowl and allow to cool, then refrigerate.

When the cake has cooled, slice it into three even, horizontal layers; sprinkle the rum evenly over each. Place the bottom layer on a serving platter and spread with one-quarter of the chilled lemon cream (if it is too stiff you can stir it briefly over heat). Add the second layer and again spread with lemon cream. Then put the last layer in place and spread the top and sides of the cake with the remaining cream.

Simmer the pistachios for 10 seconds in water and drain. Slip off the skins, chop fine, and sprinkle over the cake. Keep the dessert refrigerated until 10 minutes before serving.

Reine de macadamia

CHOCOLATE CAKE WITH MACADAMIA NUTS

My own variation on the classic *reine de saba,* this is simply a rich chocolate cake delicately flavored with macadamia nuts.

For a 9-inch (23 cm) cake:

14 ounces (400 g) semisweet
  chocolate, broken into bits
4 tablespoons instant coffee
  granules
4 eggs, separated
12 tablespoons (170 g) unsalted
  butter, at room temperature

5 ounces (140 g) macadamia
  nuts, rinsed of their salt if
  necessary
⅓ cup (40 g) potato starch
½ cup (100 g) granulated sugar
Pinch of salt

Recommended equipment: A food processor equipped with the steel blade; a 9-inch (23 cm) cake pan

Place a buttered piece of waxed paper or baking parchment in the bottom of the pan, then butter the sides well.

In a heavy-bottomed saucepan, melt 8 ounces (225 g) of the chocolate with 2 tablespoons coffee granules and ⅓ cup (¾ dL) water over low heat, stirring occasionally until smooth. Off heat stir in the egg yolks, one at a time, then return to the heat and stir until the yolks are warmed through and have thickened the chocolate slightly. Off heat again, beat in the butter by tablespoons, stirring until smooth.

Toast the macadamia nuts in a 350°F (180°C) oven for 8 to 10 minutes, until they are golden brown. With a knife, chop 5 or 6 nuts as a garnish and set aside. Pulverize the remaining macadamia nuts in the food processor, beating in the starch and ¼ cup (50 g) of the sugar when the nuts are very fine. Combine with the chocolate mixture.

Beat the egg whites with the pinch of salt until they form soft peaks. Sprinkle on the remaining sugar and continue beating until the whites are stiff. Delicately fold in the warm chocolate-macadamia mixture and pour into the prepared pan. Bake in a 375°F (190°C) oven for 20 to 25 minutes, until the cake has puffed and a knife inserted in the center comes out with only a slightly creamy layer. Allow the cake to cool on a rack for at least 45 minutes before unmolding. As it cools, it will sink into the pan and the surface will crack slightly.

Melt the remaining chocolate with 2 tablespoons coffee granules and ⅓ cup (¾ dL) water. Allow to cool slightly. When the cake is cold, invert onto a serving dish and remove the paper. Spread the melted chocolate evenly over the top and sides, and sprinkle with the reserved chopped macadamia nuts.

The cake will be best if made the day before. Keep refrigerated until 30 minutes before serving.

Le Montmorency

A VERY RICH CHOCOLATE CAKE
WITH CHERRIES

Le Montmorency is one of those chocolate desserts that is *so chocolate* that one friend of Michael's calls it "killer cake." That may be one way to describe it, but I would say that it is a dessert to satisfy any friends who love chocolate. It is made with a single layer of cake that is mostly chocolate and butter, with a mere sprinkling of flour. Once baked, the center is scooped out and mixed with a tender, thick compote of fresh cherries, and all is then spread back into the cake and simply glazed with melted chocolate. During different seasons, the cake can be made with other fruits; directions for these variations are given at the end of the recipe. To do the cake full justice, it *must* be made a day ahead, or even two or three. Then, all the flavors of chocolate and fruit will rest and ripen, and be even more rich.

For a 9-inch (23 cm) cake:

14 ounces (400 g) semisweet chocolate, broken into bits
2 tablespoons instant coffee granules
½ cup (1 dL) imported kirsch
4 eggs, separated
12 tablespoons (170 g) unsalted butter, at room temperature
⅓ cup (45 g) all-purpose flour
Pinch of salt
⅔ cup (125 g) granulated sugar
1 pound (450 g) fresh cherries or a 1-pound (450 g) can of pitted sour cherries packed in water, drained
Additional fresh cherries for garnish (optional)

Recommended equipment: A 9-inch (23 cm) cake pan

Line the bottom of the pan with a piece of buttered waxed paper or baking parchment, then spread the sides evenly with butter.

In a heavy-bottomed saucepan set over low heat, melt 8 ounces (225 g) of the chocolate with 1 tablespoon of the coffee granules and ¼ cup (½ dL) kirsch, stirring occasionally until smooth. Off heat stir in the egg yolks, one at a time, then return the pan to the heat and stir the mixture briefly until the yolks are warmed and have thickened the chocolate slightly. Off heat again, beat in the butter by tablespoons, stirring until smooth. Stir in the flour.

Beat the egg whites with the pinch of salt until they form soft peaks. Sprinkle on ⅓ cup (65 g) of the sugar and continue beating until the whites form fairly stiff and shiny peaks. Fold the warm chocolate mixture delicately into the meringue and turn the batter into the prepared pan. Bake at 375°F (190°C) for 20 to 25 minutes, until the cake has puffed and a knife inserted in the center comes out with only a slightly creamy layer. *Do not overcook.* Set the pan on a rack to cool for at least 45 minutes before unmolding. As it cools, the cake will sink and the surface crack slightly.

You can prepare the cherries while the cake is baking and cooling. Pit the fruit and set in a saucepan with the remaining ⅓ cup sugar (65 g) and 2 tablespoons kirsch. Cook over medium-low heat, partially covered, for 30 to 40 minutes, stirring occasionally. Uncover the pan for the last 10 minutes or so; the cherries should reduce to a thick compote. When done, allow to cool, then chop roughly and set aside. (If you are using canned cherries, prepare them as above, but cook them for only 20 to 25 minutes.)

Invert the cake onto a serving platter and remove the paper. Using a large spoon, trace about a 5-inch (13 cm) circle in the center of the cake, then scoop out the top part of the circle, leaving at least ½ inch (1¼ cm) of cake at the bottom. Add the scooped-out cake to the cherries and stir together well. Return the chocolate-cherry mixture back into the cake, smoothing it nicely with a flexible metal spatula.

In a heavy-bottomed saucepan, melt remaining chocolate with 1 tablespoon coffee granules, 3 tablespoons water and 2 tablespoons kirsch, stirring occasionally until smooth. Allow to cool slightly, then spread evenly over the top and sides of the cake. Use a towel dipped in hot water to remove any smudges from the platter and set the cake in the refrigerator until 30 minutes before serving. The chocolate glaze will lose a bit of its shine when chilled, but the cake is really better served slightly below room temperature. Serve the cake garnished, if you wish, with more whole cherries.

Variation: For the cherries in the recipe substitute a purée of fresh figs; or chopped dried pitted prunes or dried apricots, plumped in water and a little kirsch and flavored with orange marmalade.

Le gâteau aux pommes "Jeanina"
APPLE CAKE WITH LEMON

This is a moist little tea cake, quickly made.

For a small cake, serving 4:

½ pound (225 g) tart apples, peeled
Juice and grated zest of 2 lemons
2 eggs, separated
½ cup (100 g) sugar

4 tablespoons (60 g) unsalted butter, melted and cooled
⅓ cup (45 g) all-purpose flour
Pinch of salt
Powdered sugar in a shaker

Recommended equipment: A food processor; a 1-quart (1 L) baking dish—soufflé dish, charlotte or brioche mold, etc.

Line the bottom of the mold with a piece of buttered waxed paper or baking parchment, then butter the sides well. Quarter the apples and core them. Slice thinly and sprinkle with half the lemon juice.

Working either in the food processor or by hand, blend together the lemon zest and remaining juice, egg yolks, ¼ cup (50 g) of the sugar and the melted butter. Add the flour and beat until smooth. Beat the egg whites with the pinch of salt until soft peaks are formed. Sprinkle on the remaining sugar and beat until the whites form stiff peaks. Fold in the egg yolk mixture, then the apples. Turn into

196

the prepared mold and bake for 35 to 40 minutes in a 375°F (190°C) oven. Cool for ½ hour before unmolding onto a serving dish. Remove the paper, sprinkle with powdered sugar and cut into slices.

X

Le gâteau des Acadiens

LIGHT CHEESECAKE WITH MAPLE SYRUP,
ALMONDS, AND HAZELNUTS

This is a French-Canadian dessert traditional at holiday time. It is only slightly sweet, with the delicate flavor of maple syrup.

For a 9-inch (23 cm) dessert:

1 recipe *pâte sublime,* page 213
1½ ounces (45 g) *each* almonds
   and hazelnuts or 3 ounces
   (90 g) almonds
½ pound (225 g) cream cheese
   at room temperature, broken
   into 3 or 4 pieces
3 eggs plus 1 extra egg white

1 cup (¼ L) sour cream
¾ cup (1¾ dL) maple syrup
3 tablespoons (45 g) melted
   butter
2 tablespoons potato starch
½ cup (60 g) raisins or currants
¼ cup (½ dL) bourbon

Recommended equipment: A food processor equipped with the metal blade; a 9-inch (23 cm) springform pan

Prepare the pastry and chill it briefly. Roll out two-thirds of the dough into a 13- to 14-inch (35 cm) circle; it shouldn't be too thin, about ³⁄₁₆ inch (½ cm) thick. Fit the dough into the springform pan, tucking it gently against the sides and making a nice border. Set in the freezer for 15 minutes.

    Meanwhile pulverize the nuts in the food processor or, in small amounts, in an electric blender. If using a processor, add the cream cheese, the eggs and extra egg white, sour cream, maple syrup, melted butter and starch and beat until smooth; then turn into a mixing bowl. (Or beat the ingredients together in an electric mixer.) Place the currants or raisins and whiskey in a small saucepan and bring to a simmer. Remove from the heat and allow the raisins to macerate a few moments; then stir the raisins and whiskey into the cream-cheese mixture.

To help keep the chilled pastry shell from collapsing while baking, line it with waxed paper and weight with dried beans. Bake in a 400°F (205°C) oven for 8 minutes to firm up the pastry. Remove the beans and paper, prick the bottom all over with a fork, and bake for 8 to 10 minutes more. Remove from the oven and allow to cool.

Roll out the remaining pastry, and cut out about a dozen strips to make a lattice top. Pour the cheese mixture into the partially baked shell, then crisscross the strips of pastry over the filling, trimming the ends as necessary. Return to a 400°F (205°C) oven, and bake for 15 minutes, then lower the heat to 350°F (180°C), and continue baking for another 15 to 20 minutes. Allow to cool before carefully removing the sides of the pan and placing the dessert on a serving platter.

The *gâteau* will be best served tepid, but can also be eaten cold.

La tarte aux pommes de St. Tropez

BRIOCHE WITH APPLES AND CREAM

This light brioche is really a kind of coffee cake, ideal for teatime or a very pampered breakfast. The soaking with cream halfway through the baking gives a moist and delectable result.

For a 9-inch (23 cm) brioche:

1 recipe *jet brioche,* page 213
1 pound (450 g) tart apples, peeled, cored, and thinly sliced
2 tablespoons (30 g) unsalted butter

⅔ cup (125 g) granulated sugar
½ cup (1 dL) heavy cream
1 teaspoon vanilla extract
Powdered sugar, in a shaker (optional)

Recommended equipment: A 9-inch (23 cm) cake pan

Make the brioche dough, and while it rises you can prepare the fruit. Spread the apple slices in a single layer on a baking sheet, dot with the butter, and bake in a 375°F (190°C) oven for 15 to 20 minutes, stirring them up occasionally. The apples should be very tender. While still warm, toss them in a bowl with ⅓ cup (65 g) of the sugar.

Lightly butter the cake pan. When the brioche has at least doubled in bulk, punch it down and place on a lightly floured surface. Knead the apples and sugar into the dough, then pat it into the pan to fill the bottom. Cover with a towel and set in a warm place to rise until at least doubled in bulk; the dough should more than fill the pan. Bake in a 400°F (205°C) oven for 15 minutes. Mix the cream with the vanilla and remaining sugar. Prick the surface of the partially baked brioche all over with a fork and *gradually* pour on the cream mixture, helping the brioche to absorb the liquid with further pricks of the fork. Return to the oven, lower the heat to 375°F (190°C), and continue to bake for another 15 to 20 minutes.

Allow to cool on a rack for at least 30 minutes before unmolding and cutting into wedges. If you wish, serve sprinkled with a little powdered sugar. The brioche will be best served warm, and can be reheated.

Soufflé rocambole aux poires

SPECIAL PEAR SOUFFLÉ

This is a nice and easy dessert, if you have one ripe pear on hand.

For 4 to 6:

1 tasty ripe pear, peeled	4 eggs, separated
¼ cup (½ dL) imported kirsch	Pinch of salt
⅓ cup (45 g) all-purpose flour	½ cup (100 g) granulated sugar
1 cup (¼ L) milk	Powdered sugar, in a shaker

Recommended equipment: A 6-cup (1½ L) porcelain soufflé dish

Quarter the pear and remove the core. Cut into slices ⅓ inch (¾ cm) thick and sprinkle with a tablespoon of kirsch. Butter the dish well and sprinkle with sugar.

Place the flour in a small, heavy-bottomed saucepan and add the milk gradually at first, to make a smooth paste, and then more rapidly. Whisk over medium heat until the mixture boils and has thickened. Off heat stir in the egg yolks, one at a time. Then stir in the remaining kirsch. The soufflé base or *bouillie,* may wait for 2 or 3 hours at room temperature, with a piece of plastic wrap pressed directly onto its surface.

Beat the egg whites with the pinch of salt until they begin to form soft peaks. Sprinkle on the sugar and continue beating until a firm and shiny meringue is formed. Rewarm the *bouillie,* if necessary, and delicately fold it into the beaten whites.

Spoon one-third of the soufflé mixture into the prepared dish. Add half of the pear slices, standing them on end (if they lie flat they will prevent the soufflé from rising). Add half of the remaining soufflé mixture and the remaining pears, and top with the last of the soufflé mixture. Bake in a 400°F (205°C) oven for 20 minutes, or for 3 or 4 minutes longer if you like a soufflé with a slightly firmer center. Sprinkle with powdered sugar and serve.

Petits biscuits à l'orange

LADYFINGERS FLAVORED WITH ORANGE

These are very simple little cookies that are dry enough to hold their shape when molded with the *biscuit glacé au sorbet rose* on page 186 and are also good served with any ice cream or custard dessert.

For about 30 ladyfingers:

3 eggs
⅔ cup (120 g) sugar
Grated zest of 2 oranges

1¼ cups (165 g) all-purpose flour
½ cup (50 g) powdered sugar in a shaker

Recommended equipment: An electric beater; a pastry bag fitted with a ½-inch (1¼ cm) plain round tip

Place a sheet of waxed paper on a large baking sheet; butter it well, dust with flour and shake off the excess.

Beat the eggs with the sugar and orange zest at high speed for 5 or 6 minutes until the mixture is very fluffy and pale lemon-colored. Beat in the flour at low speed, mixing just until well blended. Scrape the mixture into the pastry bag and pipe 4-inch (10 cm) strips in neat rows onto the prepared baking sheet. Sprinkle heavily with the powdered sugar, then turn the pan upside down and tap lightly to remove any excess. Bake in a 375°F (190°C) oven for 12 to 15 minutes, until the cookies are lightly golden. Remove to a rack to cool, using a spatula. The *petits biscuits* will keep for several weeks in a tightly closed container.

La Marquise enrubannée

UNMOLDED CHOCOLATE MOUSSE WITH
COFFEE-FLAVORED WHIPPED CREAM

A *marquise* was an old-fashioned dessert mold resembling a parasol, and although that pretty mold is now rather obscure, it seems a fitting name for this rich chocolate mousse, which can be molded in a variety of ways: a *charlotte* works well, of course, or even a metal mixing bowl, which I myself use quite often. The mixture is made with Italian meringue, which makes a very creamy base for the chocolate and butter. Although the most elegant version of this dessert finishes with a peak of whipped cream, it can be done more informally with a *crème anglaise au café,* coffee-flavored custard sauce. The *Marquise* is also very festive for a birthday.

For 6 to 8:

10 ounces (285 g) semisweet
   chocolate, broken into bits
4 tablespoons instant coffee
   granules
4 eggs, separated
12 tablespoons (170 g) unsalted

   butter at room temperature
⅔ cup (125 g) granulated sugar
Pinch of salt
⅔ cup (1½ dL) heavy cream
½ teaspoon vanilla extract
2 tablespoons powdered sugar

Recommended equipment: A 2-quart (2 L) charlotte mold (or other metal mold—*not* a ring); an electric mixer; a pastry bag fitted with a star tip

Line the bottom of the mold with a piece of waxed paper or baking parchment. Melt the chocolate with the coffee granules and ¼ cup (½ dL) water in a heavy-bottomed saucepan set over low heat, stirring occasionally until smooth. Off the heat stir in the egg yolks, one at a time, then return the pan to low heat and stir for a minute or two until the egg yolks are warmed and have thickened the chocolate slightly. Remove from the heat and beat in the butter by tablespoons, stirring until smooth. Set aside.

Boil the sugar and ¼ cup (½ dL) water in a small saucepan for 1 to 2 minutes, until it cooks to the thread stage; the syrup should just run in a sticky stream from the tip of a metal spoon. While the sugar is cooking, beat the egg whites with the pinch of salt until they are beginning to form soft peaks. Gradually pour the boiling sugar in a thin stream onto the egg whites, beating at high speed. Continue beating the meringue for 4 to 5 minutes, until it has cooled and is shiny and firm. You can speed this up by setting the bowl over ice.

When the meringue is ready, fold in the tepid chocolate-butter mixture and turn into the prepared mold. Chill in the freezer for at least 4 to 5 hours—until the dessert is firm. It may wait in the freezer for a day or two.

To garnish and serve the dessert, whip the cream with the vanilla and powdered sugar until stiff. Spoon into the pastry bag. Run a flexible metal spatula around the edge of the chilled dessert and unmold it onto a serving platter. Peel off the waxed paper. Pipe the *Chantilly* as lavishly as you wish onto the *Marquise,* which, once garnished, may wait for up to an hour or two in the refrigerator before serving.

Les Ambroisies

PETITS FOURS WITH APRICOT AND
TOASTED ALMONDS

The base for these *petits fours* is a *génoise* with almonds, perfumed with kirsch.

For 25 petits fours:

7 ounces (210 g) almonds
8 tablespoons (115 g) unsalted
   butter at room temperature
¾ cup (140 g) granulated sugar
4 eggs
½ cup (1 dL) imported kirsch

¼ cup (35 g) all-purpose flour
   sifted with ⅔ cup (90 g)
   potato starch
1½ cups (3½ dL) apricot jam,
   melted and strained
5 ounces (140 g) sliced almonds,
   lightly toasted

Recommended equipment: A food processor equipped with the metal blade; a 9-inch (23 cm) square cake pan; 25 fluted paper baking cups, about 2 inches (5 cm) round

Line the cake pan with waxed paper or baking parchment and butter the bottom and sides well. Pulverize the 7 ounces of almonds either in the food processor or by small amounts in an electric blender. Then, working either in the processor or by hand, beat in the butter and when well blended add the sugar, eggs, and 3 tablespoons of the kirsch. Add the flour and starch and mix until smooth. Pour into the prepared pan and bake in a 375°F (190°C) oven for 35 to 40 minutes; the cake should be beginning to shrink from the sides. Allow to cool for 15 to 20 minutes, then unmold onto a rack. Peel off the paper and allow to cool completely.

    When cold, slice the cake into 2 even horizontal layers and moisten with the remaining kirsch. Spread one-third of the apricot glaze over the layers. Sandwich the layers together and chill, if necessary, until firm. Slice into 5 strips, then cut each strip into squares. Paint each square on all sides with the remaining glaze, and roll in the almonds. Serve in the fluted cups.

The *petits fours* will keep easily in the refrigerator for a day or two.

Les petits Bourbons

GLAZED CHOCOLATE COOKIES

These nice little cookies come from a well-worn notebook of my mother's, with absolutely no explanation for the title. They contain no liquor of any kind.

For 36 cookies:

¾ cup (100 g) all-purpose flour
Pinch of salt
½ cup (100 g) sugar
2½ tablespoons (18 g) unsweetened cocoa
6 tablespoons (85 g) cold unsalted butter, cut into pieces

2 egg yolks
1 teaspoon vanilla extract
4 ounces (115 g) semisweet chocolate, broken into bits
1 tablespoon instant coffee granules
4 or 5 pistachios, shelled

Recommended equipment: A food processor with the metal blade

Working either by hand or in the food processor, mix together the dry ingredients, and then blend in the butter. Add the egg yolks and vanilla extract and work until the mixture masses together. Press into a ball. Wrap with plastic, and refrigerate until firm, at least 30 minutes.

On a well-floured board roll out the dough ¼ inch (¾ cm) thick. Cut into 1½-inch (4 cm) rounds and place on a lightly buttered baking sheet. Re-form any scraps of dough into a ball, chill briefly if necessary, and roll out again. Bake the cookies in a 375°F (190°C) oven for 12 to 15 minutes. Place on a rack to cool.

Melt the chocolate with the coffee granules and 3 tablespoons of water over low heat, stirring occasionally until smooth. Simmer the pistachios in water for 10 seconds, slip them out of their skins and chop fine. When the cookies have cooled, glaze each with a bit of the chocolate. Sprinkle with the pistachios before the chocolate is set.

Les pommes de terre au chocolat

LITTLE COCOA "POTATOES"

These amusing *petits fours* are easily made if you have some stale *madeleines* or *génoise* on hand, but if not, there are directions here for a simple sponge cake. The cake is blended with almonds, egg and rum, then shaped, rolled in cocoa, and stuck with bits of almonds to resemble little sprouting potatoes.

For 24–28 petits fours:

For the sponge cake:

6 tablespoons (85 g) unsalted butter at room temperature	⅔ cup (90 g) all-purpose flour
½ cup (100 g) sugar	½ teaspoon baking powder
2 eggs	1 teaspoon vanilla

For the "potatoes":

Stale cake or sponge cake, crumbled	1 egg
⅓ cup (65 g) sugar	¼ cup (½ dL) dark rum
5 ounces (140 g) pulverized almonds	½ cup (60 g) unsweetened cocoa
	1 ounce (30 g) slivered almonds

Recommended equipment: An 8-inch (20 cm) cake pan; a food processor or electric mixer

Place a buttered piece of waxed paper or baking parchment on the bottom of the pan, then butter the sides well. Working either with the food processor or electric mixer cream the butter and sugar, then beat in the eggs. Beat the flour and baking powder into the butter mixture along with the vanilla. Spread into the prepared pan and bake in a 375°F (190°C) oven for 20 to 25 minutes, until the cake has puffed and is beginning to shrink from the sides of the pan. Turn onto a rack to cool for at least 2 hours, and preferably overnight, to allow it to dry out.

To make the potatoes, beat the crumbled cake with the sugar, pulverized almonds, egg and rum, either in the food processor or with the mixer, until a thick mass is formed. Pack the mixture into a small mixing bowl, and chill for at least one hour, until firm. With the help of a spoon, scoop out bits of the mixture and shape into rough oval shapes to resemble little potatoes. Roll in the cocoa and poke here and there with the slivered almonds. Keep chilled until ready to serve. The cocoa potatoes can be presented in fluted paper baking cups if you wish.

Basics

Pâte à croustade

Pâte sublime

Jet brioche

Pain de mie au lait

Nouvelle sauce verte

Fondue de champignons à blanc

Sauce tomate vite faite

Herbes de Provence

Bouquet garni

Les pâtes

PASTRY DOUGHS

One of the first things asked of me by students in any cooking class is pastry making. And they are right—this is one of the most useful basic skills of a good cook. So here are three new formulas containing my recent discoveries and preferences for certain doughs.

There are two versions of short paste with whole egg, *pâte à croustade,* one made with all butter and the other with mostly margarine. For a slightly sweet pastry, the *pâte sublime* is a fine dough made with cream and baking powder, which give a very delicate result, ideal for fruit tarts and *petits fours*. All three of these doughs are easily produced in the food processor, and although I normally recommend first mastering pastry by hand, the processor is indeed a breakthrough in the search for good and easy dough making. I must note that the flour for these recipes should be spooned into the measuring cups and then leveled off with a knife.

Pâte à croustade

SHORT PASTE WITH WHOLE EGG—FOR QUICHES, QUICHETTES, PIZZA, ETC.

For about 1 pound (450 g) pastry (enough for two 8- to 9-inch [20–23 cm] shells):

2 cups (260 g) all-purpose flour
1 teaspoon salt
10 tablespoons (140 g) cold
   unsalted butter

1 whole egg beaten with 1
   tablespoon water

Recommended equipment: A food processor equipped with the metal blade

If you are working with the food processor, place the dry ingredients in the bowl and blend them for 2 to 3 seconds. Cut the butter into 2-tablespoon (30 g) chunks, add to the bowl, and process for 8 to 10 seconds, until the mixture is thoroughly blended. Then add the beaten egg through the pour-spout with the processor running: the mixture should mass together, after a few seconds, into a slightly damp ball (if there is any dry mixture left at the bottom, beat in a few more drops of water). If you are working by hand, place the dry ingredients in a mixing bowl and stir them together. Cut the butter into small bits with a knife and blend it into the flour, using either a pastry fork or pastry blender or the tips of your fingers, until the mixture has some-what the texture of oatmeal. Gradually work in the liquid ingredients and form the dough into a ball. If the dough seems dry or if there are any unblended bits of flour left in the bowl, add a few more drops of water: the dough should be slightly moist, but not sticky, when you poke your finger into the center of the ball. Turn the dough out onto a lightly floured surface and knead for 10 or 15 seconds with the heel of your hand, pressing bits of pastry along the working surface, to complete the blending.

If you must, roll the dough out immediately, although if it seems very soft or if it is an especially warm day it would be best to firm it up in the refrigerator. If you choose to chill the dough or save it for a later use, divide it evenly in two, dust lightly with flour and wrap securely in plastic wrap to prevent it from drying out. Refrigerate for at least ½ hour, or you may store it for 3 or 4 days.

Variation: Pâte à croustade II—bonne santé (Short pastry with margarine).

2 cups (260 g) all-purpose flour
1 teaspoon salt
2 tablespoons (30 g) unsalted
  butter

8 tablespoons (115 g) unsalted
  margarine
1 whole egg beaten with 1
  tablespoon milk

Prepare the pastry as in the master recipe.

Pâte sublime

DELICATE SWEET PASTRY DOUGH
WITH CREAM

For about 1 pound (450 g) pastry (enough for two 8- to 9-inch [20–23 cm] tart shells):

2 cups (260 g) all-purpose flour
½ teaspoon salt
2 tablespoons granulated sugar
1 teaspoon baking powder

10 tablespoons (140 g) cold
  unsalted butter
6 tablespoons heavy cream
  beaten with 1 egg yolk

Prepare the pastry according to the instructions for *pâte à croustade,* either with the food processor or by hand, using any extra drops of cream necessary to hold the pastry together. Store the dough in the same way.

Jet brioche

SIMCA'S HIGH SPEED BRIOCHE DOUGH

This *jet brioche* goes very quickly indeed with the food processor and twice the usual amount of yeast, and even by hand is faster by far than the classic way. It is made with melted butter so the tiresome step of kneading softened butter in bit by bit is eliminated. Also, I only give the dough one rising before it is shaped, and this does seem sufficient since it will rise again in the pan before it is baked. The brioche, then, takes only about 3 hours from start to finish, a gain in time of about two-thirds over the traditional version. The food processor cannot do all of the kneading—indeed, what it actually accomplishes is the simple

213

blending of the ingredients, with the real kneading still taking place by hand. The dough could be kneaded in an electric mixer with a dough hook, but it is so small an amount, it is almost lost in the bowl.

Use this dough for any sausage or pâté mixture *en brioche*—such as the *saucisson de foies de volaille* on page 155; for any kind of fish or meat wrapped in pastry; and for certain desserts. It is also delicious simply baked as a bread—either with the traditional *tête* (little knob on top) as described in *Mastering the Art of French Cooking* (Volume II), or in a plain loaf tin—and served toasted and buttered for breakfast.

For about 1 pound (450 g) dough:

2 cups (260 g) unbleached all-purpose flour, more as necessary

2 packages active dry yeast, dissolved in ¼ cup (½ dL) warm milk with a pinch of sugar

1 teaspoon salt

1 tablespoon granulated sugar

3 eggs, at room temperature

8 tablespoons (115 g) unsalted butter, melted and cooled

Recommended equipment: A food processor equipped with the metal blade or special bread-dough attachment; a metal pastry scraper

If you are working with a food processor, place 1½ cups (200 g) of the flour, the liquefied yeast, salt, sugar, eggs, and butter into the bowl. Beat the mixture for 8 to 10 seconds, then scrape down the sides to incorporate any dry bits of flour. Beat the mixture for another few seconds, until the dough is smooth.

Turn the dough (which will be very soft, almost a batter) out onto a working surface spread with ¼ cup (30 g) of the remaining flour, sprinkle on the last ¼ cup flour and begin to knead the dough lightly with the fingertips of one hand, scraping and turning the dough with the pastry scraper in the other hand. As the dough absorbs the flour it will gain more body, and you can begin to knead it more firmly. Continue kneading for 3 to 4 minutes, lifting and slapping the dough roughly, and adding more flour as needed—1 or 2 additional table-spoons; the dough should be rather elastic and still quite soft, and yet only slightly sticky when it pulls away from your hand and the working surface.

If you are working by hand, place 1½ cups (215 g) of the flour, the salt, and sugar in a mixing bowl; stir the dry ingredients together to blend them. Beat the liquefied yeast with the eggs and butter. Pour the liquid ingredients into the bowl and work them into the flour. Turn the dough out onto a floured working surface and knead as in the preceding paragraph, incorporating the remaining flour.

When the dough is ready, place it in a 2-quart (2 L) metal bowl and cover the top with plastic wrap to keep the dough from drying out. Place a towel over the bowl and allow the dough to rise in a warm place—about 75°F (24°C)—or in a *buin-marie* whose water is maintained at about 95°F (35°C), until the dough has at least doubled in bulk. This will take about 1 hour.

Deflate the dough and it is then ready to use. You may wrap it tightly in a kitchen towel dusted lightly with flour and then tie it tightly with string like a plump sausage, to keep it overnight in the refrigerator, where it will expand only slightly.

X

Pain de mie au lait

FIRM TEXTURED WHITE BREAD

This is my own abbreviated version of the white bread that is so good for special little sandwiches, certain desserts—a *charlotte aux pommes,* for instance, where sautéed bread forms a crisp casing for the thick applesauce—and it is also delicious for the traditional canapés that accompany many dishes, such as the eggs *en meurette* on page 5, or the French rarebit on page 94. For breakfast, too, it is very good; one morning I was amazed to find that my dear and rather particular dog, Phano, would even eat it plain, with no jam or butter! A high compliment indeed . . .

The dough can be made in an electric mixer equipped with a dough hook or by hand (a whole pound of flour is really too much for the food processor to handle efficiently). A nice touch is the addition of a small amount of butter or margarine to the dough, which helps keep the bread moist for several days.

The instructions call for only one rising of the dough, in the pan, which gives a nice bread with a medium-fine texture. If you wish a finer bread, you can allow the dough a preliminary rise in the mixing bowl, set in a warm place until nearly tripled in bulk, about 1½ hours. Then punch down and proceed with the instructions.

For a 1½-pound (675 g) loaf:

1½ cups (3½ dL) milk, warmed slightly	2 teaspoons salt
2 packages active dry yeast	4 tablespoons (60 g) butter or margarine, at room
1 teaspoon granulated sugar	temperature
3¾ cups (480 g) all-purpose flour	

Recommended equipment: An 8-cup (2 L) bread pan; an electric mixer equipped with a dough hook (or a metal pastry scraper if you are working by hand)

Place ¼ cup (½ dL) of the milk in a small bowl and sprinkle the yeast and sugar over. Set in a warm place—75° to 80°F (24°–27°C) —until it has thoroughly dissolved and is foaming slightly.

If you are working with an electric mixer, place 2¾ cups (350 g) of the flour in the bowl with the salt, remaining milk, the dissolved yeast, and optional butter or margarine. Knead the mixture at medium speed for 3 to 4 minutes, gradually adding the remaining flour and scraping down the sides of the bowl as necessary. The dough is ready when it gathers itself into a smooth and elastic ball and cleans itself off the sides of the bowl. (If you are working by hand, stir together the flour and salt in a mixing bowl. Make a well in the center and pour in the yeast mixture, then stir in the remaining milk and butter or margarine, working at first with a wooden spatula or a fork and then with your hands. Knead the dough on a lightly floured surface for 5 to 6 minutes. It will seem fairly moist, and you can add small amounts of extra flour—a tablespoon or two, if needed—until it is smooth and elastic and only slightly sticky.)

Shape the dough and turn into the lightly buttered pan, cover with a towel and set in a warm place. Allow to rise until ½ inch (1¼ cm) or so above the edge of the pan, about 1 hour. Bake in a 400°F (205°C) oven for 45 minutes, or until the bread is a light brown and has pulled away slightly from the edges of the pan. Allow to cool in the pan, then turn out onto a rack to finish cooling. Store in an airtight container when it is cold.

The *pain de mie* freezes very well.

Nouvelle sauce verte

SIMCA'S HERB MAYONNAISE WITHOUT EGG

A kind of mustard mayonnaise without egg, which I wrote about in my last book, this sauce deserves to be repeated because it can be made so successfully in the food processor. It allows you to serve a mayonnaise-type sauce when you might otherwise not wish to serve anything with egg, for reasons of menu balance or of diet. With the help of the processor, the making of this sauce becomes child's play: the emulsion of oil and mustard, stabilized with cold evaporated milk, is perfect every time and *will not curdle*. Something, too, that is very exciting is the way this sauce becomes a *sauce verte,* green with herbs. Normally, one must chop the herbs very fine, but in this new version the whole herbs are added to the finished sauce right in the processor. I have used this sauce, then, throughout this book, when normally a mayonnaise would be called for, and it is also one that keeps much better than a mayonnaise. (I once had some in my refrigerator for two weeks.) You can make *nouvelle sauce verte* with any good fresh herbs you have. Although the recipe calls for fresh basil, which is what I have most often in my garden, even parsley together with dried herbs can give a

217

good result. Naturally, the basic sauce can also be made plain, with no herbs at all.

For 1½ cups (3½ dL) sauce:

3 tablespoons strong, creamy Dijon mustard, such as Amora or Maille
1 tablespoon good wine vinegar
2 tablespoons water
1 cup (¼ L) oil—half olive oil and half tasteless salad oil
2 tablespoons *cold* evaporated milk

1 teaspoon capers, well drained
A good handful of parsley sprigs, washed and thoroughly dried
A dozen or so large fresh basil leaves or 1 teaspoon dried tarragon
½ teaspoon salt
Freshly ground pepper

Recommended equipment: A food processor equipped with the metal blade

Blend the mustard, vinegar, and water together in the food processor, then beat in the oil in a thin stream through the pour-spout, alternating each 4 or 5 tablespoons of the oil with drops of the cold milk. When you have added all of the oil and milk, scrape down the sides of the bowl and add the capers and herbs. Beat the mixture for 8 to 10 seconds more, scraping down the sides as necessary, until all of the capers and herbs are well chopped and incorporated into the sauce. Correct the seasoning. The *sauce verte* done in the food processor is virtually foolproof, but if at any point it begins to separate, you can always bring it back by starting again with a little mustard (1 or 2 teaspoons) in a clean bowl of the food processor and gradually beating in the turned sauce alternately with an additional teaspoon or so of cold evaporated milk. (To make the sauce by hand, proceed as for a mayonnaise, beating the oil and evaporated milk gradually into the mustard and vinegar—omit the water—and adding the chopped herbs and capers at the end. If the sauce ever becomes too thick or begins to separate, beat in a small piece of ice.)

The sauce may be stored for several days or even a week in the refrigerator. To thin it down at any point, stir in a few drops of lemon juice, or water if the sauce is already acid enough; more milk will tend to thicken it.

Variation: Sauce mousseline (Herb mayonnaise with whipped cream). Beat ¼ cup (½ dL) heavy cream until it is stiff and fold into the finished *sauce verte*.

Fondue de champignons à blanc

CREAMY MINCED MUSHROOMS

This preparation of mushrooms is suitable in recipes calling for a *duxelles* and is somewhat less complicated to do. The cooking in evaporated milk gives a creamy result and helps keep the mushrooms white.

For about ¾ cup (1¾ dl.):

½ pound (225 g) firm white mushrooms, washed and trimmed	1 teaspoon salt
	Freshly ground pepper
⅔ cup (1½ dL) unsweetened evaporated milk	Freshly grated nutmeg

Recommended equipment: A food processor equipped with the steel blade; a 10-inch (25 cm) nonstick skillet

Slice the mushrooms in the food processor or with a knife and place them in the skillet over medium heat. Toss or stir for 3 to 4 minutes, until they are beginning to render their water, then add the milk and seasonings and simmer for 10 to 15 minutes, until the mushrooms are tender and the milk is thick and creamy. Chop fine in the food processor. The mushrooms will keep for 2 or 3 days in the refrigerator with a piece of plastic wrap pressed onto the surface.

Sauce tomate vite faite
QUICK TOMATO SAUCE

If the sweetest fresh tomatoes are not available, this carefully flavored sauce, made with tomato paste, is a quick and very satisfactory alternative.

For 1⅓ cups (3¼ dL) sauce:

5 tablespoons olive oil
1 tablespoon minced shallots
½ cup (1 dL) tomato paste
1⅓ cups (3¼ dL) chicken
   broth or water
1 bay leaf

2 teaspoons *herbes de Provence*
   (see below)
Salt to taste
Freshly ground pepper
Freshly grated nutmeg

Heat the olive oil in a medium-sized saucepan, add the minced shallots, and sauté gently for about 1 minute. Stir in the tomato paste, the liquid, and the herbs and season lightly. Simmer for 12 to 15 minutes, stirring frequently. Remove the bay leaf and correct the seasoning. The tomato sauce can be stored for 2 or 3 days in the refrigerator (even longer if you used only water), or for several weeks in the freezer.

Herbes de Provence

Herbes de Provence is a mixture of the herbs most frequently found in that southern French province. Dried thyme, oregano, marjoram, and savory ground with a small amount of bay leaf is the most familiar blend and is the one I prefer. Many food shops in the United States now carry *herbes de Provence* imported from France, but a mixing of your own fresh or dried herbs will do as nicely.

Bouquet garni

Although a *bouquet garni* can consist of any combination of herbs, my preference throughout this book is a collection of parsley, bay leaf and thyme. If the thyme is fresh or in sprigs, then the three herbs can be tied into a "bouquet" with string; if you are using loose, dried thyme, then you will want to tie the herbs in cheesecloth.

Index